1

“Heart of a Heroine is a bo

Thomas McQuade

“One of the biggest takeaways from my many conversations with Nancy was receiving God’s gift through knowing who I am, and who He created me to be. I was able to see how many of my past experiences mirrored my current relationship with the Lord, and how I could be set free from those patterns, and be the best version of who He created me to be. I learned to receive His love, which He so freely and willingly gave me. He has given me the desires of my heart, maybe not in the way I had imagined but in a deeper and more intentional way that only a loving God knows how to do. He sees the holes in my life (sometimes in very painful ways) to ultimately get me to where He wants me in glorifying Him through my life.
This is the message of this book. I know it will encourage women in the same way that I have been encouraged.” Candace Brians

“When I first met Nancy, 36 years ago, I was sitting in a parking lot in my car ready to leave church. I had just given my life to Christ after going through a difficult marriage that ended in divorce. I had a 3 1/2 year old son at the time. Nancy was warm and I immediately felt her genuine concern and interest in my life. I always found a listening ear and guiding loving counsel. Nancy has this uncanny ability to ask the right questions and to help me come to conclusions that are right and helpful without ever making me feel judged. She has always encouraged me to trust in the Lord’s word and in His faithfulness to work in my life. I know this book has been developing for years in her heart. It is such a joy to read and consider the principles she has written about, and look back at the story of my life, and be able to confidently affirm that God is the author of my story. The more I have surrendered to him in all the difficulty, the more I have had victory. Many of these things I learned from Nancy. She showed me Jesus in ways that spoke to my heart and helped me find victory in Him. She always pointed me to Him and His word. She was very purposeful in this. Her counsel didn’t come from her own ideas of God but from solid biblical truth.”

Denise Harrell

CONTACT INFORMATION

WEBSITE: www.heartofaheroine.com

EMAIL: heartofaheroine@gmail.com

HEART of a HEROINE

Knowing your
identity and destiny in Christ
by understanding yourself.

By
Nancy Albao

Cover design by Tamra Gerard
Cover photo by Jenna Joseph Photography

WestBow Press books may be ordered through booksellers or by contacting:

WestBow Press
A Division of Thomas Nelson & Zondervan
1663 Liberty Drive
Bloomington, IN 47403
www.westbowpress.com
1 (866) 928-1240

ISBN: 978-1-9736-4565-8 (sc)
ISBN: 978-1-9736-4564-1 (e)

Print information available on the last page.

WestBow Press rev. date: 2/6/2019

DEDICATION

This book is humbly dedicated to Jesus Christ, who is the Way, the Truth and the Life.

This book is dedicated to my precious husband, Clint, who was my lover, encourager, and best friend for 54 years. He is now in the presence of our beloved Savior. It is his unconditional love, and his unceasing commitment to affirm and respect me that have given me the confidence to reach my goal and finish this book.

This book is dedicated to my 23 favorite people in this whole world- my 7 wonderful children, my 7 beautiful sons- and-daughters-in-law, and my 9 amazing, gorgeous grandchildren. They all are the joy and fullness of my life.

ACKNOWLEDGEMENTS

First of all, I want to thank my heavenly Father for creating me and giving me life. I want to thank my savior Jesus, for saving my soul by dying on a cross for me, so that I will live forever with Him. I want to thank the Holy Spirit, who is our Comforter and Counselor, for revealing Jesus to me, for protecting me, comforting me, and making me continue to grow in my faith until my life on this earth is done. Without God, this book, and all the truths written in it, would not exist.

I want to thank my son, Jace Daniel, for being the inspiration behind the heroine theme. As a brilliant storyteller and writer, he has taught me the powerful concept of the "Hero's Journey" in literature. I will continue to learn from him as I attempt to craft this jewel in my writing. Thank you, son, for being my teacher.

I want to thank my lovely daughter-in-law, Milena, (Jace's wife), for her meticulous and gracious gift of editing my manuscript. This favor has been vitally important to what you see in these pages.

I want to thank my prayer team of eight faithful friends of many years, who have held me up and covered me with prayer when I was overwhelmed, scared, busy, tired, technologically challenged, and yet hopeful, throughout this process of writing a book. They have listened patiently, cared compassionately, encouraged, loved, and believed in me. Truly, they have done what the Bible tells the body of Christ to do for each other. Thank you my forever friends.

I want to thank the pastors, teachers, writers, theologians, and other servants of Christ that have ministered to me and made me grow. Some are friends, others are in the ministry, some I have never met, and some lived long ago, but their works are still read.

What I have gleaned from them over the last 50 years is embedded in my heart forever.

Finally, I want to thank all you wonderful friends and family who are too numerous to mention here. You have read my manuscript in all its humble and frustrating stages, you have given me more feedback and encouragement than I could have hoped for, your advice has always been to build up, rather than to tear down, and you have helped me cross the finish line!!!

Finally, I thank the people at Westbow Press for their patience with a fledgling author.

Dear Reader,

This book is dedicated to you. This is a book about you. It is about God's love for you. It is a book about what He wants to do in your life. It is a book about how His number one desire for you is that you experience His love for you, the grace He has to pour on you, and His faithfulness to care for you. It is a book about your purpose, and the hope that is found in knowing Him and following His Son, Jesus Christ. It is about the glorious experience He wants you to have with Him, as you live the life He has given you. Jesus said, "I have come that they may have life, and have it to the full." John 10:10.

He is saying that to you.

Contents

INTRODUCTION

Dear Friend,

Since you are reading this, I want to start off by telling you why I wrote this book you are holding. I have wanted to write this book for forty years, so it has been a long time in coming. This desire started when I met Jesus Christ, my Savior. When He entered my life and saved me, He also introduced me to His word. As a result, I began the transformation process that all of His children go through. Because of His forgiveness, He has given me a new life, and a new heart. He has filled me with hope, peace, trust, purpose, and joy.

First, I will share my story that led to this book. I graduated from college with a degree in Psychology. I had always been interested in people, relationships, human behavior, communication, marriage, parenting, etc. Two weeks after graduation, I married my high school sweetheart. I thought I was prepared for marriage, but, in a very short time, realized that my husband and I were not equipped to face the trials and realities of life. We had a lot to learn, and a lot of growing to do.

Two years into my marriage, I began to realize that I had a deep hunger in my soul for something more than the life I was living. In spite of our problems which almost ended in divorce, I was a happy wife to my husband, and a happy mother with our precious son, but I was empty. One lady I knew shared the gospel of Jesus Christ with me and I knew I wanted to pursue knowing more about this Christian life. I began attending a church that preached the gospel, that believed the Bible is God's word, and that Jesus is the Son of God. After a few Sundays, the message of salvation penetrated my mind. God loved me into His heart, and I knew that I wanted to live my life for my Savior and Lord.

Immediately, I was hungry for God's word. I wanted to know everything it said and how that would relate to me and my life. I wanted to know Jesus, and that knowledge only comes through the word of God. As I began studying, I found that His word spoke about so many topics and issues that we had discussed and studied in psychology. That should not have been surprising to me, because psychology is the study of human beings. In fact, the Greek word for soul is psyche. Psychology means the study of the soul.

The Bible is The Book that tells humans beings about their soul. I was excited to see how the two subjects would tie things together for me in my mind. I was sure that psychology (and all my college studies) would verify God's word and bring it to life. It didn't take long for me to realize that God's word is supreme over all other beliefs, philosophies, theories, intelligence, religion, opinions, ideologies, principles of thought etc. All other ideas and theories and explanations of life are man-made, but God's word is inspired, and given to us by our Creator for the sake of our soul.

God began to teach me about myself and others through His word. His word became relevant to every issue of my life. And it answered questions and guided me through life in a way that no other ideas could. It met me at the most important moments of my life, whether it was times of joy and happiness, or at times of deep sadness, fear, insecurity, disappointment, guilt and regret. And it proved to me that Jesus is who He promises to be, and is faithful to love and care for me in a way that I could never have imagined.

Because of this, I want to share His truths with you. I want you to know Him in a way that will transform you. I want you to understand yourself, and what causes you to make the choices and decisions you make, and how your world-view determines so much in your life. I want you to hear His voice in your heart as He leads you through your life.

The world we are living in today is in desperate need of the life Christ came to give us. He died for you to be forgiven and free, filled with hope and purpose. He wants you to rest in His love instead of exhausting yourself as you cope with your problems, relationships, and your past, present and future.

God has changed my life from who I was 48 years ago when I first met Him. He has spent 48 years teaching me His ways, His wisdom, His answers to life, and now I want to help other women who are hurting, struggling, and fearing life because they do not know that there is hope. We have it ingrained in us that we have to be independent and strong, that we can't trust anyone, and that life has no purpose. I have been mentoring women in these truths, in one-on-one conversations and biblical counseling for many years. It has been my joy to repeatedly witness the breakthrough a woman experiences when the Holy Spirit, who is our Counselor, helps her to make the connection between knowing her own mind and heart, and understanding how God is working in her life to give her victory in her problems, and hope for her future. When we believe Him and His word, He is always faithful to do this. Based on the many miracles I have seen in women, I want to spend the rest of my life telling women that God is faithful, and He will never, ever leave them. If we believe Him and trust Him He will bring us through victoriously.

In this book, we are going to find out what the Bible teaches us about our heart. What does the heart of God's heroine look like? How does she think? How did she come to think the way she does? How does she grow? How does she learn about God? How does she face life? How does she become the woman God created her to be? How does she learn to trust God, and live out the story He is telling about Himself through her life?

Praise God that His Word holds the answers to all these questions. The Bible teaches us everything we need to know about ourselves, and about God, so that we can have the heart of His heroine.

In this book, each chapter examines a specific aspect of our heart. Join me as we see what God has to say to us.

Take It To Heart:

"The purposes of a person's heart are deep waters, but one who has insight draws them out." (Proverbs 20:5)

"Above all else, guard your heart, for everything you do flows from it." (Proverbs 4:23)

CHAPTER 1

Heart Of A Heroine

"Heroine: The central female character in a story"
Dictionary.com

"I am a heroine, not because of the great things I do, but
Because of the great things
God is doing in me."

God is an Author. In fact, He is The Eternal Author. He creates stories. He doesn't just write stories, as human authors do. He makes the stories happen in real life and His characters are real people. Like any author, He always has a heroine in His story. Your life is one of His stories, and you are the heroine that He has created to live out that story. You are perfectly designed to be His heroine of the story He is telling through you. And He is the Hero.

What is His purpose? It is to show the world through you what He is like. As you believe Him, love Him, trust Him and follow Him, the events and lessons you go through show the world that God, whom you trust, is faithful and good. The Bible is filled with stories about real people who lived real lives. Each of their stories tells us something about God, because the Bible is about

God. God did not stop telling stories when the Bible was written. He has been telling stories all through history. As the Author, He tells a story through each of us, because "we are His handiwork, created in Christ Jesus to do good works, which God prepared in advance for us to do." (Ephesians 2:10)

J. R. Tolkien, the author of Lord Of The Rings, is considered to be one the greatest storytellers in British history. He was a devout Christian and had a passionate love for the Gospel as a historical fact and as the greatest story ever told. He said many profound things about what stories are and how they affect us as humans.

In a conversation with C. S. Lewis, who was an atheist and materialist at the time, he explains that mythical tales, such as Lord of the Rings, contain all the elements of what humans long for. They picture a world that is supernatural in which they can escape from the natural world as we know it, where death is final, power is in the hands of the wicked, and evil triumphs. In those myths "the supernatural is real, love is eternal and overcomes death, and good triumphs over evil. Victory is snatched from the jaws of death, and the hero, through unselfish sacrifice, brings life and resurrection. They are stories of joyous deliverance and happy endings. Human beings crave these stories because deep down we know that, There <u>is</u> something wrong with this world, good <u>should</u> triumph over evil, and we are <u>not meant</u> to die. Myths point us to a deeper reality that has all the elements that the material world lacks, and that our hearts long for." J.R. Tolkien https://www.youtube.com/watch?v=WoAE15gtEzg.

This brilliant Christian storyteller continues. "The Gospel of Jesus Christ is the greatest epic, because it actually happened. It is supernatural <u>and</u> it is history. Jesus actually lived. He became flesh and lived with us, day to day. He knows our weaknesses and can sympathize with us. Like all heroes, He literally laid down His life for us as He was nailed to a cross. Victory was snatched from the jaws of death by the Resurrection. He defeated our enemy, and

Good triumphed over evil. He IS the HERO of History. History is His Story. His sacrificial death and resurrection punched a hole through the concrete wall that stands between life as it is and life as it was meant to be. His story is not one more wonderful story that points to an underlying reality. Rather, Jesus is The Reality to which all other stories point."

He then goes on to say that God is still telling stories. He states, "We tell stories because God is a storyteller. We tell our stories with words. He tells His Story with History. And we are part of His Story."

Now, God lets us participate in His Story. We are a character in His Drama. Acts 17:24-27 tells us, " The God who made the world and everything in it is the Lord of heaven and earth and does not live in temples built by human hands. And He is not served by human hands, as if He needed anything, because He Himself gives all men life and breath and everything else. From one man He made every nation of men, that they should inhabit the whole earth; and He determined the times set for them and the places where they would live. God did this so that men would seek Him and perhaps reach out for Him and find Him, though He is not far from each one of us. For in Him we live and move and have our being."

As Tolkien taught, stories are the means by which people pass down their values and traditions to the next generations. That is God's design. The stories we read in the Bible tell of heroes that demonstrate our virtues and flaws as humans. God's purpose in His stories is to inspire us to know Him and live for Him. Throughout His word, we read of real people and how God revealed Himself to them and worked in them, and how they loved Him.

God has designed our minds to be shaped by the stories we hear and tell. "We are all storytellers. We all live in a network of stories. There isn't a stronger connection between people than storytelling," Jimmy Neil Smith, Director of the International Storytelling Center

God still reveals Himself to the world through His people. It is your story that puts flesh and blood on God's truth. It is your testimony of what HE has done in you that He uses to draw someone to believe in Him. And it is your life that He uses to tell another story of His love and truth. It is a unique story. It is your story.

Unfortunately there is a big difference between our story and a fiction story. Unlike the heroines in stories written by man, who do exactly what the author writes that they will do, we don't always want to live the story that God is writing. Because we are human, and we were born sinful creatures, we now have a heart that doesn't want God to write our story. Each of us has a will that wants to write our own story and choose for ourselves what we want our life to be. This is a tragedy, because the most wonderful story we could ever live is the story God created us to live.

But there is good news. God sent Jesus to save us from our independent, sinful will, so that He could give us a new heart, the heart of His heroine of the story He wants to tell through you. It is never too late to ask Him to give you a new heart.

Your story did not begin when you gave your heart and life to Christ. It began before the foundation of the world. We are not God's heroines because of our accomplishments and righteousness. We are His heroines because He created us to glorify Him. We are always growing and changing as we surrender our lives and hearts to Him. We give up our pride and self-righteousness, and our stubborn will and exchange it for His resurrection power living in us. Everything about us, our successes, failures, desires, dreams, and brokenness, is all part of our story. He uses ALL of our experiences to tell His story.

Take It To Heart:

"My people, hear my teaching; listen to the words of my mouth. I will utter things we have heard and known, things our ancestors have told us. We will not hide them from their children; we will tell the next generation the praiseworthy deeds of the Lord, His power, and the wonders He has done, so the next generation would know them, even the children yet to be born, and they in turn would tell their children. Then they would put their trust in God and would not forget His deeds, but would keep His commands." Psalm 78:1-4; 6,7

CHAPTER 2

Vanity Fair

Who of us is happy in this world? Who of us has
what he desires- and having it, is satisfied?
William Thackeray, Vanity Fair

Throughout history, empires have risen and fallen, cultures have thrived and then ceased. There have always been the rich, the poor, the powerful, the weak, the proud and the humble. There have been times of peace and of war. Some have endured famine, plague and annihilation, while others have prospered in wealth and luxury.

King Solomon of Israel, who lived 3,000 years ago was known all over the world for his wealth and kingdom. He said of himself, "I denied myself nothing my eyes desired; I refused my heart no pleasure." (Ecc. 2:10) And yet his commentary on all his wealth was summed up in the first verse of his Book of Ecclesiastes:

"Meaningless! Meaningless! Everything is meaningless!!" (Ecc. 1:2)

Solomon's words are as profound a critique of our time as they were of his. Human nature and cultures have never changed. As Solomon said, "There is nothing new under the sun." (Ecc. 1:9)

One country song puts it like this.

"They say, hey, it's only human to never be satisfied.
Well, I guess that I'm as human as the next one. Just as soon as
I get what I want, I get unsatisfied. Oh,
I keep looking, I keep looking,
I keep looking for something more.
I always wonder what's on the other
side of the number two door.
Yeah, I keep looking, looking for something more."
"I Keep Looking" Sara Evans, 2000

Compared to generations ago, we are living in the most materialistic culture we have ever seen. Girls and women of all ages are persuaded by clever marketing schemes to collect the latest trends, from trinkets to technology. The more luxuries and pleasures that the world offers us, the more we are driven to acquire material things. We are defined by our outward appearance and our possessions. Women of every age are self-conscious of the process of ageing and are spending exorbitant amounts of money to slow it down. The virtues "inner beauty" and "growing old gracefully" are irrelevant and obsolete.

This river of materialism is resulting in tragic consequences. Emotional and mental health is threatened. Anxiety, depression, addiction, perfectionism, loneliness and suicide are of epidemic proportions. Psychologist Madeline Levine, a practicing psychologist for 25 years, recently has observed and reported in her article, The Price of Privilege, that "The various elements of a perfect storm--materialism, pressure to achieve, perfectionism, disconnection--are combining to create a crisis in America's culture of affluence."

Materialism is more than a desire for material possessions. It is a philosophy that states that everything that exists in the universe is matter. There is no spiritual realm or reality. The only reality that exists is what we can experience with our five senses. There is no basis for spiritual ideas and values. There is no truth to build our life on, no purpose to live for, and no hope for the future.

In chapter 1, we read of J.R. Tolkien's conversation with C.S. Lewis. He tells Lewis what the materialist philosophy has done to us. "We have been duped into accepting the first real lie of Materialism. That is the hideous claim that there is no supernatural. The materialists have imprisoned us in a world of mere matter. They have made us believe that this is all there is. - 3 dimensions, 5 senses, and 4 walls. The four walls of materialism are the fours walls of a prison, and the materialists are our jailers."

We need to understand that in any culture, the prevailing worldview of the day influences all aspects of a person's life. Our hope is that God will teach us how to resist those influences and walk in His truth.

It should not surprise us that in this materialistic generation we are also desperately searching for love, peace, and fulfillment. It bears witness to the fact that the spiritual world is real, because of our spiritual longings that go beyond the material world. We are trying to meet our spiritual needs with material solutions.

Like a thirsty traveler in an arid desert, searching desperately for an oasis, we are pursuing what turns out to be nothing but a shimmering mirage on a distant horizon. Around the banks of this mirage, the world has set up its tents of attractive merchandise and enticing wares, bidding the traveler to come, buy, drink, and be filled. When these allurements and promises fail to quench the thirst in our hearts and give rest to our tired souls, we realize that the mirage was a deception and there is no water to drink. The promises we have believed leave us empty. Our souls are wounded and bruised.

What "in the world" is going on?

What is the impact on women of this epidemic of spiritual thirst and hunger in our culture? Is there a plague in our society that only God can cure? When we look around us, we see heartbreak everywhere. Marriages are wounded, homes are shattered, dreams are ripped away. Men, women, and children of every age are caught in the crossfire of the battle we fight. The cause of this heartache is deception. It creeps into our lives insidiously clothed in harmlessness, disguising its poisonous venom. A teenage girl, who desires to be thin and popular, copes by spending her lunch hour in the high-school bathroom, vomiting so she won't gain weight. A young career woman, wanting to have fun and be accepted in certain social circles, gets trapped in a world of alcoholism and drug addiction. A lonely girl, in search of love and security, goes from one abusive relationship to another, leaving her with an unraveled string of broken, meaningless, sexual relationships, and abortions. She wonders if there is an answer for the guilt and emotional devastation that results. A mother, wanting to get back into shape after a few pregnancies, decides to work out at a gym and finds herself attracting the exciting attentions of a new man, and is caught in the undertow of adultery and divorce. The successful, independent woman, in seeking prestige, power, and influence, ends up in a dizzying whirl of stress, insomnia, anxiety, and burn-out that must be treated with drugs. The creative homemaker wishes to remodel her beautiful and expensive home with the luxurious decorations that fill the furniture stores and home-dec websites, but ends in a collision with debt and financial ruin. These nightmares can throw women into an abyss of hopelessness and despair. All of us have experienced part of this nightmare, or know and love someone who has. Surely such sobering facts should warn us that money and material things do not give us what we need and want.

What "in the world" is the matter with you?

The deepest longing of our soul is to know the eternal God and Creator, who knows us because He made us. He knows every thought we have ever had or ever will have. He knows our every need, every wish, every desire. He knows that He is the only One who can fulfill us and satisfy all our needs. His eternal love for us is the only love that is perfect, undistorted, and complete. He has created us for eternity, and our hearts hunger for beauty and purpose that last forever. He knows that when we set our affections on possessions that are temporary, and we invest our lives in dreams that are fleeting, we will become disillusioned, discontent, and unsatisfied. That disillusionment will lead to an unending search for satisfaction and fulfillment. Until we desire Him, and He quenches our heart's thirst with the Living Water, Jesus Christ, our heart will be fickle, impulsively flitting from one illusion to another, only to discover that each one is a brittle treasure, crumbling before our eyes like jagged fragments of once precious jewels, now devoured by the past.

What escape is there from this strangling spiral of desire and disappointment? Is there nothing but a mirage in this spiritual desert in which we find ourselves? Is there no cure for our sick soul, no water for our parched life? Is there no oasis from which we can drink? As Christian women, we are not immune to this disillusionment. The temptation to find fulfillment in these worldly promises is creating a struggle in our souls. We are torn between our desire for the world's treasures, on the one hand, and our love for the Lord on the other. The tension between these two opposing forces is choking out the peace and joy the Lord came to give us.

What happens to a culture that removes God from its thinking and attempts to fulfill every desire with material goods and man-made solutions? What happens to a woman who tries to satisfy her spiritual needs for love, joy, and peace, without God, without His son, Jesus, and without a relationship with Him? It is a recipe for gaping emptiness and spiritual disaster.

What "in the world" are you going to do?

We live in the most self-centered generation in American history. Pride, arrogance and self-centeredness are admired as virtues to be cultivated and imitated. God's ways are mocked, ridiculed, and despised. In order to find peace and fulfillment, we must recognize that the influences to join this river of materialism and self-indulgence are sapping our joy and endangering our very existence as God intended us to live. Jesus spoke of money and wealth more than He did of heaven and hell. It is for our soul's sake that we must take His words seriously, embrace His message in the deepest part of our hearts, and apply them to each choice and decision we make.

God makes this very clear in His word. In Deuteronomy 30:11, 14, God tells His people, "What I am commanding you today is not too difficult for you or beyond your reach. No the word is very near you; it is in your mouth and in your heart, so you may obey it." In verses 19 and 20, He says, "I have set before you life and death, blessings and curses. Now choose life, so that you and your children may live, and that you may love the Lord your God, listen to his voice, and hold fast to him. For the Lord is your life."

Who "in the world" are you going to believe?

Do you want to get off this glossy merry-go-round of deception that keeps you going around in an endless cycle of ups and downs, repeating the same disappointments and heartaches, never moving forward, never making any progress in life? Do you want to find peace and contentment in your soul, and eternal purpose in your heart?

The answer is found in Jesus Christ, the Son of God, who came to this earth to make you whole, to forgive you for all your sins, and to save your soul which is infinitely precious to Him. He died so that you would have life. He promises in His word:

"Now this is eternal life: that they may know you, the only true God, and Jesus Christ, whom you have sent." (John 17:3) "For my Father's will is that everyone who looks to the Son and believes in Him shall have eternal life." (John 6:40)

Dear reader, He had you in His mind and heart before He created the universe, before anything existed. He is offering you eternal life today, through His son, Jesus Christ. And He is inviting you to come to Him and receive all that your heart needs, that this materialistic culture can never give you.

Take It To Heart:

"All of us followed the ways of this world. We lived among them at one time, gratifying the cravings of our flesh and following its desires and thoughts. Like the rest, we were by nature deserving of wrath. But because of His great love for us, God, who is rich in mercy, made us alive with Christ even when we were dead in transgressions. For it is by grace you have been saved, through faith, and this is not from yourselves. It is the gift of God- not by works, so that no one can boast. For we are God's handiwork, created in Christ Jesus to do good works, which God prepared in advance for us to do." Ephesians 2:2-5; 8-10

CHAPTER 3

Hall Of Mirrors

"Who is this girl I see
Staring straight back at me?
When will my reflection show
Who I am inside?"
Disney Movie, "Mulan"

PART I

A True Story

Sharon is a beautiful woman. She was raised in an atmosphere of beauty and fashion. She was one of four beautiful sisters, living in southern California. She had all the things society valued. She never went anywhere without looking her best. Her hair was perfectly styled and colored at all time. Her makeup was applied flawlessly every morning before she left the house. She had never lacked for anything that money could buy.

Sharon had a problem. She was the only one of these four women who struggled with her weight. She often asked God,

"What were you doing when you gave me these genes. Even my identical twin sister doesn't have a weight problem! Why Lord?"

She grew up in a Christian home and attended a large, prosperous church, made up of other beautiful, sophisticated women. She always wore the latest styles and was a trendsetter among her friends.

She met and fell in love with a tall, dark, handsome, successful man. She gave birth to four daughters. She lived in a lovely home in the heart of a thriving community. Her daughters were the joy of her life.

Life was good.

As her daughters became teenagers, she noticed that her clothes were getting too tight. Her striking blonde hair, which had always been her crown of glory, was thinning in places. When she looked in the mirror, she saw more lines around her mouth, her eyelids were beginning to sag, and her neck was showing signs of the toll gravity was taking on her body. When she turned on the T.V., every show was about having a makeover. At her computer, all the pop-up ads showed pictures of some woman feeling miserable because of her aging skin, with the promise that you could buy a product that would change all that.

One day, sitting in the shop waiting to get her hair highlighted, she picked up a brochure advertising all the amazing treatments and products to make women look younger. She put it in her purse. Getting home, she read it thoroughly. It sparked a desire in her. After all, women were able to do all sorts of things to improve their appearance and erase the damage left by time. She was feeling frumpy. She needed something to lift her spirits. She would make a phone call in the morning.

By the next afternoon, she had made dozens of phone calls getting prices for tummy tucks, face lifts, hair extensions, glycolic peels, permanent makeup, a full-body lift- everything that is offered to the woman who wants to cling to her youth and preserve her beauty. When she added it all up, she looked at the total, which amounted to thousands of dollars.

As she sat at the table, she felt an unsettling lump in the pit of her stomach. Why was she feeling convicted about how she had spent her day? She had never seen anything wrong with taking care of herself before. Was it the Lord tugging on her? She did not have peace in her heart. She shoved all the brochures into a pile on her desk and left them there.

That evening, before bed, she took out her Bible. She turned to some of her favorite verses that had comforted her heart so many times before. The words from Proverbs 31:30 jumped off the page, "Charm is deceptive and beauty is fleeting; but a woman who fears the Lord is to be praised. (Proverbs 31:30)

Her heart bowed in gratitude to Christ. Oh Jesus, forgive me for being caught up in what the world tells me to buy, a world that looks at the outside of a person, instead of the inside. I know that what I look like is not who I am. Father, please make my beauty come from your Spirit living in me. Help me to let others see Christ in me. I can't help others or show them your love just by having a makeover. I can only bless others as I show them what you are like."

She slept soundly.

The next morning started out busy. She hurriedly got herself ready for her day, rushed around making breakfast, shot out the door to take the girls to school, then hurried to do a few errands before work. She knew she would not have time to come home and freshen up but she did not have a choice

As she got into work, a posh ladies' boutique, she was stopped by one of her co-workers. "Sharon, you look so beautiful. Did you change your hair or something?"

Laughing at the irony of the question, she laughed, "Are you kidding? I've been running around doing errands."

A few hours later, her manager studied her while she arranged jewelry and handbags on the polished glass shelves.

"Sharon," she asked, "you look different. Did you change your hair or have your makeup done? You look so beautiful."

Again Sharon chuckled at the question. Surely this was ridiculous. Probable her cheeks were flushed from the heat.

When she got ready for bed that night, standing in front of the mirror, she remembered her prayer from the night before. She had not thought of it all day. She certainly did not think of it when she was complimented. Her eyes welled up with tears. "Oh Lord, you are so real, your word is so true. Thank you for teaching me something so profound and touching me with your precious spirit today."

The reality that Christ gives her inner beauty that others can see has given her a new perspective on aging. She is learning to be content and fulfilled, because she has eternal life and the unfading beauty that comes from Christ.

This story is a simple one, one that many of us can relate to. It is an example of how we often experience a conflict in our identity. Sharon was uncomfortable with what she saw in the mirror, and yet believed that her identity was not based on her outward beauty. As Christian women, we find ourselves in similar struggles. We feel the world and its values pulling us in one direction and the Lord and His ways pulling us in an opposite direction. Many of us are disillusioned in our relationship with Christ because of our weaknesses and shortcomings. Some of us feel convicted in our failure to please God but we feel trapped because we don't know the answer to our problem. We compare ourselves to other Christian women whom we perceive as more "spiritual," and then we decide that we will never measure up to the standard we have invented. These struggles rob us of the abundant life Jesus came to give us.

What do I mean by our "identity"? This term became popular as it was used in psychology. It refers to a person's self-concept, and the qualities, beliefs, personality, looks, and abilities that make up a person. It refers to the study of a person's personality, thoughts, and emotions, and what generates them. The word "psyche" comes from the Greek, which means "soul, mind, spirit, i.e. the invisible entity which occupies the physical body."

The Bible is God's word that explains all we need to know about the soul. The Bible teaches that we are made in the image of God. We have a spirit. We are not just a material being of flesh and bones. We have an eternal soul.

Psychology studies the non-material spiritual dimension of human beings. A few of the terms they use are self-concept, self-image, and identity. The Bible refers to our spiritual being with terms heart, innermost being, inner being, soul, spirit, mind, self, and the hidden person of the heart. We will be using these terms throughout this book, as we see how both the Bible and psychology are about the soul.

What psychology calls the identity, or self-concept, the Bible calls the heart. My heart is the core of my being. It generates my thoughts, motives, goals, and emotions. It is the lens through which I view my life and myself. It is the mental tape I listen to, the boss I work for, and the leader whom I follow. My heart is the executor of my will, the authority I obey, and the master whom I most want to please.

Proverbs 4:23 tells us, "Above all else, guard your heart, for everything you do flows from it. (Proverbs 4:23) How can we know what our hearts are saying to us? What are the issues that flow out of our hearts? These are questions that nag us - sometimes lightly pecking away at us, almost unnoticed, but robbing us of joy, nevertheless. At other times, they gnaw at us until life becomes tasteless and meaningless. To answer these questions, we must know what God says to us about these things. They are spiritual questions, and only God's word has the answer for our spiritual needs.

A woman's heart is a very special creation in God's eyes. He loves a woman's heart, which so uniquely expresses and reflects His attributes. The famous 19th century preacher, Henry Ward

Beecher, said, "When God thought of woman, He must have laughed with satisfaction and framed it quickly- so rich, so deep, so divine, so full of soul, power, and beauty was the conception."

God delights in making each woman unique, each with different gifts, personalities, and purposes in His plan. Women have qualities that touch the lives around them in a way that none of His other creatures do. In spite of this, many women are hurting, empty, and lonely. Many who have what the world calls happiness and success are tired and painfully disappointed with life. Even Christian women ask themselves the question, "Why do I battle the same old problems, day after day."

To those who have received Christ as their personal savior, God's word promises, "Therefore, if anyone is in Christ, [that person] is a new creation. The old has gone, the new has come." (II Corinthians 5:17) And He promises, " I will give you a new heart and put a new spirit in you." (Ezekiel 36:26)

In order to know our heart and understand ourselves and our relationship with God, we need to understand how our identity develops from the time we are born.

The Development of Our Identity

One of the most important things God has taught me is the impact my identity has on my actions and thoughts today. Even though I have been a Christian for many years, the habits I formed and the methods I rely on to live my life are still very much a part of me. Understanding myself and the influence my identity still has on me has helped me to see why I have resisted the Lord when He wants to change me. This knowledge has helped me to trust Him. He is setting me free from many old ways that robbed me of the joy and peace that He gives. As I have ministered this to women, I have seen them experience joy and victory in their lives.

Before the age of two years, we had no idea that we were an autonomous and separate individual from all the other people in our life. We had no concept that we could think and behave independently of other people. Then between the ages of one and three years, we developed self-awareness, which is the consciousness of our individuality from others. As we have learned, the Bible calls this self-awareness the heart. Our identity begins to develop as we interact with our environment, experiences, and relationships with other people. We begin to learn how to function in our little world in order to be safe, happy, and loved, which are our most fundamental needs for life.

As we consider our fundamental needs, it is important to know that God created us with these needs. The Bible calls them love, joy, and peace. They are lodged deep within our soul. He promises us, His creatures, that He wants to fulfill all our needs. He is the source of all that we need, our very life and breath itself. He is the only answer to the deepest longing of our souls. And He created us to experience His love, care, and compassion.

Our Three Fundamental Needs:

These needs are called fundamental because they are necessary for life itself. They are:

1. Safety and security

This of course is the most obvious. If our safety or security such as food, water, shelter, clothing, is threatened by starvation, thirst, extreme cold or heat, or physical danger, we could lose our life.

Jesus promises, ""Therefore I tell you, do not worry about your life, what you will eat or drink; or about your body, what you will wear. Is not life more important than food, and the body more important than clothes? Look at the birds of the air; they do not sow or reap or store away in barns, and yet your heavenly Father feeds them. Are you not much more valuable than they? So do not worry, saying, 'What shall we eat?' or 'What shall we drink?' or

'What shall we wear? Your heavenly Father knows that you need them. (Matthew 6:25,26,31)

2. Love and acceptance

Studies of actual settings in orphanages, such as in Russia, have proven in history that when a child only receives its physical needs-food, water, shelter, but not physical contact with another human being, and no relationships with people around them, they die. If they don't die, they show severe damage in intellectual, physical, and social functions and abilities. Sometimes, even when they are rescued from such deprivation, this damage is irreparable. A friend of mine adopted a beautiful girl from Bulgaria. The child had been in a crib all her life. She was fifteen years old, she could not walk, she was in a wheelchair, and she looked like she was eight years old. All of her needs for food, water, and shelter were provided, but she had not received human love and contact, which is vital to life and development.

Many of us know what it is like to live without love and acceptance. We long to fill that emptiness in some way. Many are searching, wondering if it is even possible to ever receive a love which is unconditional and faithful. We can't deny our need for love. The whole Bible, from the first word to the last is the story of God's love for you. He promises, "I have loved you with an everlasting love; I have drawn you with loving- kindness. (Jeremiah 31:3) He himself has said, "Never will I leave you; never will I forsake you."(Hebrews 13:5)

It is important to keep this in mind as we learn about our hearts, and how our identity develops.

3. Fulfillment and happiness:

This is perhaps the one need we haven't considered as a life threatening problem when it is not met. However, the lack of fulfillment and happiness, if taken to extreme is devastating and ultimately responsible for death. For example, the unmet need for happiness and fulfillment leads to depression, anger, bitterness, and loneliness. If is worsens, it progresses to despondency, hopelessness, and despair. In the end, it can be the destroyer of mental health, and the will to live, ending in suicide.

The word fulfillment refers to the fact that we become who and what we are created to be. We fulfill our purpose by developing our gifts and talents and allowing those gifts and talents to be used for good. In return for our contribution to our world, we feel that our life has significance and purpose, and we experience joy and happiness.

Charles Colton, the founder of Prison Fellowship Ministries, in his book, Justice That Restores, relates why fulfillment is a fundamental need, and how a total absence of fulfillment can be life threatening. He states,

"Christians believe and we intuitively understand that humans are created in the image of God and that God created us for a purpose. This is part of the image of God within us. We are restless until we find and fulfill our purpose. When circumstances make it impossible for us to be productive, humans can go mad, quite literally. This point was made by Fyodor Dostoyevsky, the Russian novelist, who had spent four years in a Siberian prison camp, where he experienced horrific abuse. Prisoners were forced to dig a deep hole in the ground for no reason, and then refill the hole, and then to do this over and over again. He argued that if one wanted to crush a person utterly, one should simply give him work of a completely senseless, irrational nature. ' I believe a person would hang himself, preferring rather to die than endure such humiliation, shame and torture.'"

The Bible teaches us that our greatest fulfillment and purpose is found in Him. We were created for Him. As St. Augustine said, "We were created for you, o Lord, and our hearts are restless until they find their rest in you." We were not designed to create our own purpose or fulfill our own needs and desires. We were created to live for a purpose greater than ourselves and for His glory. We were created to find our purpose in the eternal, not the temporal. Jesus said, "I am the good Shepherd. I have come that [you] may have life, and have it to the full, " (John 10:11,10)

This whole subject about our needs and our purpose are summed up in one verse. Jesus calls out to us, "Seek first, His kingdom and His righteousness, and all these things [that you need] will be given to you as well." (Matthew 6:33)

How Do Our Needs Motivate Us?

Each of us has a vital need to maintain our ideal, safe, healthy internal and external environment. We set a guard over ourselves. Like the watchman on the wall, we constantly know if, "all is well." It is a feeling of peace, well-being, and comfortableness, both physically and emotionally. The biological term for this is homeostasis. When this balance is disturbed, we sense our need, and are motivated to meet that need, or find a way to have it met. We can feel the need through our internal environment, such as hunger, thirst, insecurity, anxiety, emotional or physical pain, and discomfort, or our external environment, such as danger, deprivation, hostility from others, or adversity.

Here is an example of how this principle works. Picture yourself sitting on the sofa some evening, relaxing after a long day. (Even this action is meeting the need for rest, to relieve tiredness.) The silence is broken by the sound of your stomach growling. Your state of being filled is disturbed by hunger pangs, and you want to eat. You are then motivated to interrupt your comfortable, relaxing time and go to the kitchen and get a snack. This is because your need for food is stronger than your desire to relax. Later this same evening, you are still sitting on the sofa watching TV and a cold breeze comes through the window and you get goosebumps and you shiver. Now you are motivated to get up from your comfy spot and go get a sweater.

These are simple illustrations of how our internal and external environments, when they are not balanced, cause us to sense a need and motivate us to meet that need. As life gets more complex so do our needs. We often feel more than one need at a time and experience conflict because they cannot both be met. For example, a teenager is told to be home at a certain hour, but she wants to be with her friends. She must choose between having peace with her parents or the acceptance of her peers. As we grow up, we decide what is important to us, and what choices we must make to meet our needs.

Whenever our comfort and equilibrium is out of balance, we want to do whatever we need to do to be comfortable again. The more intense the need is, the stronger the motivation is to meet that need. In Psychology this principle is called "hierarchy of needs." This drive is one of the strongest forces in our identity development. When we were little, we learned how to interact with our world in order to maintain our balance by getting what we wanted and needed.

Our identity, as we have seen, is our unique combination of personality traits, internal resources, and coping methods for dealing with life and getting our fundamental needs met. Psychology has long discussed and studied the Nature vs Nurture debate. They discuss the question of whether a person's identity is the result of heredity (Nature) or environment. (Nurture) Is our identity a product of genetic makeup? How much of a our identity is shaped by the influences of people, relationships, experiences, and social environment. The emphasis is on the environmental influences on the person. In contrast, as we learned in Proverbs 4:23, the deciding factor in determining our identity is our heart, with which we choose how to deal with life and take care of ourselves.

God created us to be shaped by Him. He gives us His desires and His thoughts. As we have a relationship with Him, He shapes our identity and because of that, we desire to be like Christ. When our hearts are surrendered to Him, we are made whole. We live for Him, not ourselves. We live the life He created us to live, a life of joy, peace, purpose, and fulfillment in this life and for all eternity.

Our Identity As Little Girls

When we were little girls, we absorbed information from our environment and processed it in our minds. We learned that there was a big world around us, and that we wanted and needed to fit into this world. We experienced many sensations and emotions. We observed that there were other people in our world. We found that they responded to us in various ways. They were mirrors to us. We learned our value from their responses, and their treatment of us, and what characteristics were acceptable and what were not. We discovered if we were cute or clever, pretty or plain, athletic or uncoordinated, intelligent or stupid, outgoing or shy, weak or strong, loveable or annoying, and the list goes on. The people in our world taught us what traits were valued, and what we needed to do to acquire those traits. We knew from their reactions and comments if we possessed or lacked the valued traits. All of this processing lead us to make choices about how we would function in our world in such a way that we would feel safe, accepted, loved, comfortable, and happy.

Of course this is an academic description of personality development. As little girls, we were not consciously thinking in these terms. We were jumping rope, riding our bicycle, climbing trees, playing with baseballs or dolls, or dressing up in lipstick and big dresses, and clopping around in high heels. But the process was going on, just as physical growth goes on, without us thinking about it. This process can be demonstrated through positive or negative behavior, healthy or unhealthy habits, and functional or dysfunctional methods. The process does not imply success or failure, or right or wrong behavior. It refers to how we developed methods that in our mind worked so that we were able to get what we wanted and needed. We were created by God with this drive to survive. And it is one of His greatest gifts to His creatures.

The choices we make and the conclusions we draw from the consequences of those choices help to shape our identity, which is in a continual process of development. We go through seasons and stages. When we were very young, we were primarily influenced by our parents, siblings, an aunt or uncle, a grandmother or grandfather. Then when we went to school, teachers and friends played an important part. In high school, for many of us, peers and cliques had more influence on us than parents and teachers. This is more common now than in previous generations. As adults, we are influenced by our husband, children, in-laws, friends, and co-workers. All through life, new people, places, and experiences make their imprint on our soul. We continue to respond to these experiences, and add the new information to our identity.

As we grow into womanhood, we know what our personality traits are and how other people perceive us. Deep in the core of our soul, we know our innermost thoughts, dreams, weaknesses, failures, fears, and sins. We carry our identity with us wherever we go. It is the silent voice that dialogues with us from day to day, for the rest of our life. Regardless of whether or not other people in our life know how we see ourselves, we act and respond to all life experiences that come our way on the basis of our identity.

PART II

Who I See In The Mirror

As mentioned earlier, the Bible calls our identity our heart. The writer of Proverbs tells us how important this part of our being is in determining our actions and choices. Proverbs 4:23 tells us to guard our hearts because it is in our heart that we deal with all the issues of life that face us.

Proverbs 27:19 points out, "As water reflects a [woman's] face, so a [womans's] heart reflects the [woman]."

Ever since woman could see her reflection in a mirror, she has had the mistaken notion that her face and outward appearance reflect who she is. This is why we put so much emphasis on beauty, youth, and our image. This is why we are so influenced by the opinions- approval and disapproval- of people. We believe what the mirrors in our world tell us, whether that mirror is made of glass or human flesh. This is a problem for two reasons:

- The world we live in is a fallen world. Each of us, as well as every other person we know are sinners. We are all human and flawed. The people in our world do not know us totally, as God does. Their opinions are based on their own perspectives, experiences and needs. They are fickle and unstable. Like the wind, they are always changing.
- As this verse in Proverbs tells us, we are mistaken in thinking that our identity is what we see in the mirror. On the contrary, our identity flows from our heart.

This verse in Proverbs make me think of a hall of mirrors in a circus. The mirrors are distorted reflections. They can make you look short and fat, or tall and svelte. I find that I would rather look into the mirror that makes my short, stubby fingers look long and tapered, my waist trim, my belly flat, my figure tall and willowy, and my fat ankles to be delicate and emaciated.

Like the hall of mirrors, the people in our lives are mirrors that are distorted. The reflection they give is inaccurate. And this works both ways. Like the hall of mirrors, which can make you look better or worse than you are, people may give us too high or too low of an opinion of ourselves. And we must realize that we ourselves are also distorted mirrors to others. We will never really know ourselves, or the purpose for which we are created if our identity is based on the shifting opinions and fickle approval of an unpredictable world.

In the Disney movie, "Mulan," the young Chinese girl sings a profound song. She is gazing into a still pond of water and sees the reflection of her face. In a poignant, earnest plea, as if she knows that something is amiss, she asks,

"Who is this girl I see, staring straight back at me. Somehow I cannot hide who I am, though I've tried. When will my reflection show who I am inside."

Have you ever asked yourself that question? Deep down in our heart, we know that there is a unique person who wants to fulfill her purpose and become who she was created to be.

God -The Perfect Infallible Mirror

Our God-given identity is not a product of our environment, but His creation. God's word tells us that we are made in His image. Our Creator gives each of us a unique identity in order to reflect His image. His plan for each of us is perfectly suited to the identity He designed for us-our gifts, talents, physical characteristics, and personality traits.

The Bible tells us that because of sin, we are spiritually dead without God's son, Jesus Christ. We are separated from the Source of life. The umbilical cord has been cut, and our souls are alienated from God, the Father of all. God's exquisite design has been damaged beyond recognition. Sin has devastated our soul and deformed our identity. Jesus Christ came to earth to save us from sin and its ravaging effects. He died on a cross, not only to take the punishment that we deserve, but also to heal our souls and restore our identity to His original design.

In order to be healed in our identity, each of us must receive Jesus Christ by putting our faith in Him, through believing the Gospel. The Gospel is that Jesus Christ, God's one and only perfect, sinless Son, took the personal sins of each of us, individually and literally, upon Himself, in His body, to take the punishment our sins deserved. Each Christian who has put faith in Christ believes that:

"He was nailed to a cross because He loved me intimately and personally and wanted to purchase my forgiveness with His own precious blood, so that I could have eternal life and live with Him in heaven for all eternity. He did this because God, His Father, sent Him to save me from my sin and its devastation. He planned to save me before He even created the world. By believing this, I receive His life and I become a new creation. He doesn't improve the old me, or simply patch up the broken parts. He gives me a new nature, a new heart, a new identity."

II Corinthians 5:17 promises, "If anyone is in Christ, he is a new creation. The old has gone, the new has come".

If you have never received God's forgiveness and eternal life, you may pray right now to receive Him. You can pray:

"Dear God, I know that I am a sinner and have been separated from You all of my life because of it. I believe that You sent Your beloved Son, Jesus, to die on a cross for me. I believe that Jesus' sacrifice and the shedding of His blood paid for the punishment I deserve and that my sins are completely washed away. I ask You, Jesus, to come into my heart and make me new. I believe You have done this because You love me, and not because of anything I have done to deserve it. I accept Your forgiveness and the new heart that You give me. I thank You that You have done this and that You give me a new life. I thank You that You are going to change me to make me more like You everyday until I am in heaven with You for all eternity. Amen."

You Are A New Creature In Christ

At the moment you receive Christ, you begin a new life in which you become who you were created to be. Because He is the perfect mirror-faultless, undistorted and perfect- He is the One who now begins to mold your identity, the identity for which He created you. You no longer have to be shaped by the influences and expectations from an imperfect world. He knows everything about you and loves you completely, in spite of your sins, faults, and mistakes. It is His perfect love that transforms your identity. It is only this transforming power of His unconditional love that can make you whole and fulfilled in the deepest part of your being. Only His intimate knowledge of you can enable you to know yourself and your purpose on this earth. His love for you is food for your hungry soul, and living water for your parched and thirsty spirit.

Take It To Heart:

"O Lord, you have searched me and you know me. For you created my inmost being; you knit me together in my mother's womb. I praise you because I am fearfully and wonderfully made. Your works are wonderful, I know that full well. My frame was not hidden from you when I was made in the secret place. When I was woven together in the depths of the earth, your eyes saw my unformed body. All the days ordained for me were written in your book, before one of them came to be. Search me, O God, and know my heart; test me and know my anxious thoughts. See if there is any offensive way in me, and lead me in the way everlasting."

Psalm 139:1, 13-16, 23-24

CHAPTER 4

"Me"-andering Through Life

"Meander- To wander aimlessly, undirected"
Dictionary.com

Who is "Me?"

At the age of two years, we begin to realize that we are a separate person from our mother, father, brothers, sisters, and other people in our lives. All kinds of things are going on inside our two-year old mind. It is at this stage that our self-concept begins to develop. We become aware of our needs and how to get them met. We experience new emotions such as frustration, boredom, embarrassment, disappointment, pride, self-accomplishment, independence, and shyness. Our will becomes a strong force in determining how we act, think, and feel. It is about this time that we start going through the phase known, as "the terrible twos." It is called that because our will suddenly has the ability to act independently and clash with other people's wills, especially with parents or siblings. Suddenly the words "mine" and "no" become a regular part of our vocabulary and the "me" in us becomes the center of our world.

I can distinctly remember my first tantrum. I was only about four years old. No one has told me of this incident. I can remember clearly what was going through my mind at the time. My mother was going shopping. In those days, my mom did not have a car so she had to catch the bus. The bus stop was quite a walk from our house. I started out with her, begging her to take me with her. She had gotten a babysitter, and had no intention of taking a four year old on the bus to go shopping! Well, I was mad! In fact, I was furious. I started screaming at her to take me with her. The further we walked the harder I screamed.

I can remember to this day how loudly I tried to scream. I could not have exerted more force from my little lungs. My mother had to bolt herself up emotionally, and steel herself against my tirade. I was like a queen who had just been crossed. I may have been little, but I was bent on using my power to get my way. I can remember walking behind her, seeing the back of her head, thinking that at any moment she would cave in to my demands and turn around. Well, she was stronger than I.

As she got further away from me, I could not scream any louder. I was in disbelief. How could she ignore me, ME, the queen of my little kingdom. I finally had to give up, turn around and begin my slow, dejected trudge home. By the time I reached my driveway, my shrill wails had been humbled to weak little whimpers. At that moment, a neighbor saw me and compassionately asked me what was wrong. With a sob in my voice, I told her that my mommy wouldn't take me with her. (Of course, I could make the lady think it was my mommy's fault!) I can still remember our dialogue. She answered me by saying ever so tenderly, "I'm sorry." With all the indignation that a four year old can feel, I thought to myself, "What a stupid thing to say. Why is she sorry? She didn't do anything to me!"

Whenever I remember this experience, I understand the profound truth that I was born self-centered; that I have a strong will; and that I want my way. And this was evident at such a young age!

From the time we are about three years old, each of us is "me-"andering through life, watching out for the most important person in the world- myself. Like a phonograph record player, my "self" is the center spindle, around which everything rotates. If you have ever seen a record turning on a turntable without the spindle, you have noticed that it cannot turn properly, it is off center, and turns randomly without direction, often sliding off the turntable altogether. The spindle makes it all work right. And in my world, my self makes sure that everything in my world turns right for me, and plays my song. When my plans don't go right, my world is shaken, my will is challenged, my happiness is threatened, and my perspective is out of focus.

Unlike the record spindle, we were not created to be the center of our lives. The spindle may keep the record turning right, but when we live in self-centeredness, living for "me," our life does not move in the direction and toward the goal for which we were created. How often have we struggled with the same old problem repeating itself over and over? It feels like we are going around in circles.

The Bible tells me that "Me" is what is wrong with me. And it was for me that Jesus came to die. It was to deliver me from my self-centeredness and futile efforts to live successfully and happily. This is the good news of the Gospel. It is my prayer that in this book we can look at God's ways together and discover the glorious reason and hope we have when we believe and obey Jesus' words. He said, "If anyone would come after me, he must deny himself and take up his cross and follow me. Whoever wants to save his life will lose it, but whoever loses his life for me will find it. (Matthew 16:24,25)

A Lesson From Life

Because we are born with a God-given temperament, we each respond to life differently. God did not make us robots, or cut us out with a cookie cutter. We are made in His image and each of us is unique. As time passes, our self-concept becomes more distinct and we know we are individuals, separate from any other person.

As I have walked with the Lord, He has given me insights into how my self-concept has influenced me in profound ways.

By the time I was seven years old, I was a compliant child. I wanted to have peace and safety more than anything else, even if it meant missing out on something fun and more exciting than peace and tranquility. I could play by myself for hours. One of my favorite stories was Ferdinand the Bull. It was about a bull who was gentle and sweet and just loved to smell the flowers. He did not make a good bull for a bullfight for that reason. Instead of fighting the toreador, he just sat down in the sunshine and smelled the pretty flowers on the ladies' hats. Well that was me! I was the opposite of strong willed! I did not have a lot of self-confidence or ambition. I hated to take risks, so I avoided situations in which I could get hurt. I was even content to skate with just one skate on one foot so that my other foot could be on firm ground! The problem was I never got very far.

My father was a good man, and a strict disciplinarian. I knew he loved me, but in many ways I was afraid of him. I protected myself from his anger by being obedient. I did not want to rock the boat. I avoided getting into trouble at all costs.

These things played a big part in how my self-concept developed. My self-concept has influenced my responses to others and their opinions of me. It has directed many of my choices and decisions about my needs, my dreams, my goals, my abilities. It has determined my perspective on my life. It has been a strong factor in my walk with God, because it is the grid through which I perceive Him, His word, and His love. It has influenced my ability to trust or not to trust Him, and my willingness to obey or disobey Him. The most wonderful miracle He has done in my life is to give me a new identity by replacing my wrong thinking with His truth. He promises in John 8:32 "You will know the truth and the truth will set you free." (John 8:32) The changes God has done in me are the greatest miracles of my Christian life. He has given me more joy and freedom than I ever thought possible, because now I am becoming the person He created me to be. This process continues throughout our lives. He is never finished with us until He takes us home to be with Him forever.

As you and I walk with Him and surrender our will to His, He gives us a new self-concept that is shaped by His truth and nurtured by His love. In the following chapters, we will discuss how He does this.

We are all unique

As we look at how our self-concept developed and the traits that we possessed as a child, we can find clues to our present day behavior. We begin to understand why we hang on so tightly to certain habits and why we respond to situations the way we do. One woman will respond to her life differently than another, even in similar circumstances. We have each learned different ways that worked or failed because of our strengths and weaknesses. We have different needs and desires. What is important to one is not important to another.

When we put our faith in Christ, we bring all that we are and think into our walk with Him. Because we have different self-concepts and personalities, we respond to His Word differently. We find that parts of His Word are easier to obey because we have a natural inclination or habit to do what it says. In contrast, we realize other parts of His Word don't come naturally, and we see that we are inadequate or unwilling to obey.

Trusting in God or Yourself

As we learned in chapter 2, each of us has a self-concept which is the central force that generates our motives, goals, and plans, and our responses to the circumstances in which we find ourselves.

The Bible talks a lot to us about our self-concept. It describes the self in many places. A word study on the Bible's teaching on "self" will reveal one common thread that runs through every verse. The thread is that we, as human beings, trust in ourselves rather than God. Whom and what we trust is the driving force in our lives. Before we put our faith in Christ as our Savior and God as our Father, all of us are putting our trust in our own ability to take care of ourselves, to feel safe and loved, and to find happiness. We may not be aware of it. We may think we put our trust in people or money or other things, but at the root we are trusting in ourselves to make the decisions that concern our happiness. We think we can choose what things will provide our needs.

It is crucial to our spiritual well-being and our relationship with God that we know what He says to us about where we are putting our trust. God is passionate about His love for us, and what He has done for us. He created us to abide in Him and to trust Him for all of our needs, and to be filled with His love and joy and peace. He longs to pour out His blessings on us.

The message of the Bible is that our sin of living independently of Him and trusting in ourselves separates us from Him and His wonderful abundant love. He repeats over and over that where we put our trust determines our destiny. It is no small matter to consider.

I have been teaching women for 40 years. I have seen a light go on in a woman's heart as she views her struggles in light of her self-concept. She gains insight from these clues and the Lord uses that insight to help her to let go of trusting in herself and to put her trust in Him.

Have you ever thought about where you put your trust and the implications that it has on you? If we are going to have a meaningful relationship with God, we must answer this question.

Take It To Heart:

"Whoever wants to be my disciple must deny themselves and take up their cross and follow me. For whoever wants to save their life will lose it, but whoever loses their life for me will find it. What good will it be for someone to gain the whole world and yet forfeit their soul. Or what can anyone give in exchange for their soul. For the Son of Man is going to come in His Father's glory with His angels, and then He will reward each person according to what they have done." Matthew 16:24-27

CHAPTER 5

Where Did "I" Come From

"We all like sheep have gone astray,
Each of us has turned to our own way."
Isaiah 53:2

Where Did "I" Come From?

"Why do you spend your money on what is not bread and your labor on what does not satisfy?" Isaiah 55:2

God's word resonates in the hearts of us who know Him and believe in Christ. His questions strike at the heart of a culture built on self-esteem. We are striving with all of our time and energy to be satisfied with ourselves—physically, emotionally, and spiritually.

Like a silent searchlight, the eyes of the Lord look into our hearts and ask us this rhetorical question. He has been asking mankind this same question for 6,000 years. God asks us this so that, as we come face to face with our vanity and emptiness, we can become conscious of our spiritual hunger. God does not ask us questions because He needs to know the answer. He already knows the answer. He asks us, so that we will think about our actions, our motives, and our choices. What is our answer to His question? Do we continue to think that the things of this world can satisfy our spiritual hunger and thirst, which can only be satisfied by knowing our Creator? We fill up our time until it is so packed with activity and commitments, there is no time for a relationship with Him. We design our lives with ourselves at the center. The word "my" becomes a hashtag in our our daily planners: my schedule, my priorities, my jobs, my finances, my commitments, my house, my appointments, my family, my friends, and so on.

Yet I neglect my soul and my spiritual needs. My spirit is faint from fear, weak from stress, depressed from loneliness, bruised from broken relationships, tired from disillusionment, and hungry for hope.

Like someone who is malnourished but doesn't know it, we do not attribute these symptoms of spiritual hunger to our need for God. If God were to describe our spiritual condition in pediatric terms, He would say we are suffering from FTT, which means "failure to thrive." This term is used to describe a child who does not gain weight and develop properly because of an inability to eat or get enough food..

As human beings in our thriving and prosperous culture, we adeptly manage our lives, We faithfully consult our daily planners, but are too busy to meet with the our life's Planner. God knows that we need to ask ourselves questions like we find in Isaiah because, unless we do, we will continue down the road of futility. In this question, God is drawing us to Himself. He asks because He is offering to fill that hunger. He is the only One who can. We know this because He tell us in the two previous verses, <u>"Come, all you who are thirsty, come to the waters; and you who have no money, come, buy, and eat! Come, buy wine and milk without money and without cost."</u> (Isaiah 55:1 Notice the exclamation point that Isaiah uses.)

God is inviting us to receive the answer from Him. In honestly answering this question, we are taking a step toward Him, and the first step toward true joy.

In order to understand why we "spend our money on what is not bread, and our labor for what does not satisfy," we need to understand what the Bible says about our hearts. Without God's word, we are absolutely ignorant of our spiritual condition. We only know this world and what we can see, hear, touch and feel with our senses. We are lost and without any knowledge of God. We are destitute of truth and wisdom. We are incapable of understanding spiritual truths from God's word unless we have God's spirit living within us.

When we look for the answers to the dilemma we are in, we must go to the Bible. It tells us that we are lost and empty without the God of creation, the One who gives us life. Man has not always been in a lost and damaged condition. God did not create man to live an empty meaningless life. If He didn't, you ask, what went wrong? How did the problem start? The answer lies in the book of Genesis. It goes back to the very beginning.

Paradise Created

By reading what happened to the first woman that God created, we begin to understand why we act the way we do.

In Genesis 2, we read of God's creation of the first man. He named him Adam. After creating Adam, God said, "It is not good for the man to be alone. I will make a suitable helper for him." (Gen. 2:18) He then caused the man to fall into a deep sleep and took one of the man's ribs and made a woman from the rib he had taken out of the man. (Gen. 2:21-25)

In this beautiful paradise, the Garden of Eden, God gave them everything they needed. He told them they could eat from any tree in the garden. He gave them only one command. He said, "You are free to eat from any tree in the garden; but you must not eat from the tree of the knowledge of good and evil, for when you eat of it you will surely die." (Gen. 2:16, 17)

Adam and Eve lived in perfect paradise- absolutely no problems, nothing that could cause trouble of any kind. Can you imagine? What is your idea of perfection? The first thing that comes to my mind is that they had no problems and no heartache! It must have been wonderful. They loved God and each other perfectly. They were perfectly suited to each other. (Gen. 2:18, 20) They were in God's presence continually. They could hear the sound of the Lord as he walked in the garden in the cool of the day. They walked with Him and talked with Him as they breathed the perfumes from the flowers and tasted the luscious flavors from the fruits that grew on the trees. They were totally known and they felt no shame. God delighted in them as a father delights in his adorable children. They could see His smile and the sparkle in His eyes as He enjoyed them, for He created them for His pleasure. Worship of Him bubbled up out of them naturally and wholeheartedly as they lived in the presence of His glorious beauty and perfect love. They had no thought of wanting to disobey Him or displease Him. His Word says, "You are worthy, our Lord and God, to receive glory and honor and power, for you created all things, and by your will they were created and have their being." (Revelation 4:11) They had no fear that this would all end or that they would ever be abandoned or betrayed. Imagine a place of total security, wholehearted trust, unending love, and uninterrupted joy. No such thought of guilt, shame, betrayal, cruelty, disillusionment, or discontent of any kind. The reality of suffering and despair had not yet been born.

When we look at the world, and even at our own wicked hearts, we know that we are no longer living in the Garden of Eden. What could Adam and Eve have possibly done that would cause their world to go reeling off its God-created course, careening into a place where there is unbearable suffering and hideous evil of every kind.

Paradise Invaded

As we continue on into chapter 3, the suspense tightens, the tragedy impends, and the story takes a troubling turn. For you see, Adam and Eve and God were not the only characters in this drama.

We are introduced to a new character. He is insidious in his perverted beauty but devastatingly evil in his plan. His plan was motivated by a pride and jealousy, that was all consuming, and a hatred that was bent on revenge and destruction. This creature was Satan. He had been the most beautiful angel in God's creation. He was the worship leader for all the heavenly hosts. Because of pride, he became jealous of God and wanted to receive the worship for himself. For this sin, God cast Satan out of heaven. He gave him the earth as his palace and made him the ruler. As the day of creation dawned, Satan had a plan to destroy God's crown of creation- man. (I Peter 5:8) His scheme was to make them desire the same pride that had thrown him out of heaven, the pride of self-"I." (Isaiah 14:13,14)

Genesis describes this evil being in one word- crafty. He came to Eve as a serpent. (Genesis 3:1) He engages her in a conversation by asking her a question.

"Did God really say, 'You must not eat from any tree in the garden?'" (Genesis 3:1)

How clever. By saying the word, "really," he introduces doubt. Then when he says the word, "any," he outright misquotes the Lord in order to make Him sound harsh and unfair. He exaggerates the truth to make God appear to be unloving, strict, and stingy- wanting to withhold the best from His children.

Eve answers by restating God's command. In verse 2, she says, " We may eat fruit from the trees in the garden, but God did say, 'You must not eat fruit from the tree that is in the middle of the garden, and you must not touch it or you will die.' " (Genesis 3:2,3) Good answer, except for one thing. God never mentioned not touching the tree. That was Eve's word, not God's. And so, Satan engaged her in a conversation. He was laying the trap and she was slowly walking into it. Now he answers her statement with an outright lie and a flat denial of God's command to her. He cunningly persuades her to rethink the truth. And the result is a lie.

"You will not surely die," the serpent said to the woman. "For God knows that when you eat of it your eyes will be opened and you will be like God, knowing good and evil." (Genesis 3:4)

His words hung in the air as the woman considered this profound statement.

Could it be true? Could her life in the garden be even better than what she already had? Could she be missing out on something good and beneficial? Even worse-could God be depriving her of something that she needed or would enjoy? Is it possible that His will wasn't good, and His love wasn't perfect?

The moments tick by. Satan can wait. He lets his words take effect in her mind. He doesn't force her or even suggest that she take the fruit. He waits and lets her mind draw its conclusion and make its choice. He is subtle and clever. Too much force is too obvious. It is always more effective to let the victim believe he is making his own choices, even when that choice is the path to his self-destruction.

And so Eve did think. She looked at the tree. She thought about Satan's words. She compared them to what she already knew from God. But she drew a fatal conclusion. Verse 6 tells us, "When the woman saw that the fruit of the tree was good for food and pleasing to the eye and also desirable for gaining wisdom, she took some and ate it. She also gave some to her husband, who was with her and he ate it. Then the eyes of both of them were opened, and they realized they were naked; so they sewed fig leaves together and made coverings for themselves." (Genesis 3:6,7)

The crushing blow had been dealt. Satan smiled in triumph. Man had fallen. Their first reaction was fear and shame from their nakedness. Their first solution was to hide from God.

Paradise Lost

And so the Garden was no longer paradise. Adam and Eve could not live there any longer. In God's judgment, He cursed the land. Woman would bring forth children in pain, and man would bring forth fruit from the ground through painful toil and hardship. Their end would be death. (Genesis 3:16-1)

Paradise Redeemed

But God did not abandon Adam and Eve and mankind without hope. He told the serpent in verse 15, "I will put enmity between you and the woman, and between your offspring and hers; he will crush your head and you will strike his heel." In these words, God is promising to send His son Jesus, to defeat the work of Satan and to save man from the ravaging effects of sin. What a promise! What mercy! This is what Jesus did when He died on the cross. He crushed the devil's head and redeemed us from sin. Now, all of us who put our faith in Him are saved from our sins-the guilt and the punishment-and rescued from death and hell.

Paradise for me?

This history, written 4,000 years ago, aims at the very core of what makes each of us tick. It traces our fallen heritage back to its roots. It diagnoses the deformity of our will, the malady of our identity, and the disease of our heart.

The Bible states, "We all, like sheep, have gone astray. Each of us has turned to own own way." (Isaiah 53:6)

We have turned our backs on God and chosen to live independently of Him. We want our own way just as intensely as we want food and water. It is the most natural inclination of our hearts- looking out for Number 1, Me, myself, and I. Now my will is the driving force of my life.

Each of has turned to our own way. The ways we have chosen to go are as numerous and diverse as there are people in this world. The common denominator, though, is that we choose our way instead of God's will for our lives in order to be happy. For 6,000 years people have tried to possess everything the world offers in order to be content and fulfilled.

But without God.

And God asks, "Why do you spend your money on what is not bread, and your labor on what does not satisfy?"

God is calling to us in our spiritual hunger. He knows that we are in need of His grace, His love, and His presence. His love is deeper and higher and wider and longer than our minds can comprehend. (Ephesians 3:18) He stands with His arms open wide and His heart overflowing.

"The Lord is compassionate and gracious, slow to anger and abounding in love. He will not always accuse, nor will He harbor His anger forever; He does not treat us as our sins deserve or repay us according to our iniquities. For as high as the heavens are above the earth, so great is His love for those who fear Him." Psalm 103:8-11

Precious friend, the Lord's compassion for you, His daughter, and His passion for your eternal soul drove Him to the cross for you. We ask ourselves, "What is in 'me' that resists this incomparable love?" He invites you to seek Him, trust Him and look to Him to meet your deepest needs, for He has given you the heart of His heroine.

Take It To Heart:

"He himself bore our sins in his body on the tree, so that we might die to sins and live for righteousness; by his wounds you have been healed. For you were like sheep going astray, but now you have returned to the Shepherd and Overseer of your souls." I Peter 2:24,25

CHAPTER 6

What's So Bad About Good Self-Esteem?

"The best lies are the ones that look the most like the truth. The newest lie is the oldest lie." Nancy DeMoss Wolgemuth Lies Women Believe And The Truth That Sets Them Free

Where did we get that idea?

Living in our generation and culture, we have grown up with the idea that I must trust in myself to be a successful, productive and fulfilled person. It is referred to by the term "good self esteem." About sixty years ago, the concept of self-esteem took root in our thinking, as psychologists taught it. Before that time, it was not a common idea. For a generation, this concept has come to be accepted as a psychological truth about human behavior. There are various views and variations on what a good self-esteem is and how it is acquired. It is a concept that pervades our thinking about who we are, what our purpose in life is, and what our worth is as a human being. It relates to what the Bible calls our heart. Therefore, it is of utmost importance that we compare the world's psychological concept of good self-esteem with the Biblical concept, for there are some crucial contrasts.

It is only God's word that is the perfect truth for our lives. Our beliefs must be examined in the light of God's word, where we can see if there is any error. Any philosophy that contradicts God's word must be discarded from our thinking. Our lives must be built on truth if we are to love God with all of our hearts and possess all that He promises us. God wants us to "not conform any longer to the pattern of this world but to be transformed by the renewing of [our] minds. Then we will be able to test and approve what God's will is, His good, pleasing and perfect will." (Romans 12:2))

I received Jesus Christ as my personal savior when I was 24 years old. I had been graduated from college for two years where I majored in Psychology. When I began to learn of God's love through His word, I was amazed at how He valued me and gave me worth. Because of my psychology background, I interpreted much of God's word to me in terms that were familiar to me. For example, I looked for principles in His word that I could obey, and I felt secure in His love because I was obedient. It gave me self-esteem! This is a very shaky premise for knowing His love, and much of it was based on pride. It was not long, however, that God began to challenge my old thinking with His truth. Psychological theories either contradicted God's truth, or they lacked the essentials of truth because they left God out of the subject completely. When you study human beings but do not consider the One who created them, you have a big problem and foolish conclusions. Like a manufacturer's instruction manual, God's word teaches us to understand ourselves.

Philosophies that are only partially true are not true at all, as far as God is concerned. The opposite of truth is a lie. God warns us not to be deceived by worldly thinking. As Nancy De Moss says in her book, Lies Women Believe and the Truth That Sets Them Free, "Lies represented in what we hear today are not [necessarily] polar opposites of the truth, but distortions of the truth." We must realize that a distortion of the truth, no matter how small or harmless it may appear, is harmful to us if we believe it. Every thought we carry around in our mind has an effect on us, our actions, and our belief about God. That is why God wants us to be transformed by the renewing of our minds. (Romans 12:2)

Let's look at some of the key issues regarding the teaching about self-esteem, and hold them up to God's word for scrutiny. Unlike man's ideas and theories, which come and go and change according to popular opinion, these are the truths that have comforted believers throughout history, regardless of their generation or their cultural background, because "the word of the Lord stands forever." (I Peter 1:25)

Self-Esteem Defined

Self-esteem is defined as the "disposition to experience oneself as being competent to cope with the basic challenges of life and being worthy of happiness."

What do we notice about this definition? Does it not sound like the purpose for which we are created? Is there anything wrong with this concept when we compare it to what God says about us? As we consider it in light of God's word, we can see that it is only a description. Psychology cannot give us the answer to how to have self-esteem. This is where it fails to give us the truth that only God can give us. The two crucial questions we must ask are:

1. Does God want us to have good self-esteem?
2. How do we acquire it?

1. Does God want us to have self-esteem?

The message of the Gospel is that God loved us so much that he sent His Son to die on a cross to pay for our sins, to forgive us and to give us eternal life, so that we would live in Heaven with him for all eternity. Yes, God put eternal value on us. He loves us with all of His heart. God created us in His image to be like Him and glorify Him through our faith, our testimony, and our actions, which reflect who He is.

When we experience God's love personally, we realize our true worth for the first time. This sense of self-worth is very different from psychology's concept of self-esteem because it is the result of being loved and valued by God, not the result of our own accomplishments and competence. It is value, which He bestows on us, out of the eternal fountain of His goodness toward us. He promises to love us for all eternity. There is no fear of losing His love, because we didn't earn it or deserve it to begin with. We did nothing to convince Him to love us. "This is love: not that we loved Him, but that He loved us and sent His son as an atoning sacrifice for our sins." (I John 4:10) "[Nothing] will be able to separate us from the love of God, that is in Christ Jesus our Lord. (Romans 8:39)

In contrast, psychology tells us that:

1. Self-esteem is related to your self worth and your value. Building self-esteem is a first step toward your happiness and a better life.
2. Self esteem increases your confidence. If you have confidence, you will respect yourself.
3. Low self-esteem causes depression, unhappiness, insecurity and poor confidence.
4. Negative self-talk scares us out of taking positive risks so we can avoid failure.
5. You can build positive, self-empowering inner dialogues. Your strong sense of self-worth allows you to maintain your power.
6. Your purpose in life is about what you plan to achieve and the kind of person you want to be. The self worth you feel will determine the kind of person you can become.

Perhaps you have never had an occasion to read such statements as these, but the beliefs stated here are part of the warp and woof of our culture's worldview. They are so incorporated into our thinking as to become the very foundation on which we build all our other beliefs. This philosophy has come to be accepted as fact and as such has permeated education, child rearing, marriage, business, medicine, law, the court system, social work, sports, entertainment, etc. It has fostered pride, rebellion, self-centeredness, materialism, secular humanism, moral relativism, and ungodliness. It has taught people that they are entitled to their desires, and that they are capable of anything they set their mind to. It has pitted people against each other when they disagree, or compete to have their own way. It has had a devastating effect on our society in broken relationships. It has left thousands of men, women, and children emotionally scarred as one person has run in pursuit of his/her self-worth.

Since the year 2000, there have been psychologists who have studied self-esteem and challenged the status quo. They have proved that self-esteem does not do what is promised. In 2006, San Diego professor, Jean Twenge, published her conclusions in a book titled, "Generation Me." On the cover it said, "Why today's young Americans are more confident, assertive, entitled, and more miserable than ever before." She believes that the obsession with self-esteem has fueled the rise of depression in the United States and encourages narcissism and is undermining the skills of young people." The article makes this disturbing statement. "Self-esteem, as a construct, is a quasi-religion. Yet in the U.S., the self-esteem bandwagon rolls on unabated."

For a generation, the marketing industry has inspired women to have what they want, use their strength to get what they want out of life, and to assert themselves to a high position in their family and their world. It is saying you can have the husband and romance and the home and the children, but through pride and power, you can also have all that satisfies your own wants and desires. You can have it all!

Diametrically opposed to this, God's word tells us that "charm is deceptive and beauty is fleeting; but a woman who fears the Lord is to be praised. (Proverbs 31:30) "Your beauty should not come from outward adornment. Instead it should be that of your inner self, the unfading beauty of a gentle and quiet spirit, which is of great worth in God's sight." (I Peter 3:3,4)

I pray you will join me in taking a penetrating look at this philosophy that contradicts God's truth.

If we aren't committed to comparing the two and choosing God's truth for our lives, then we will be led astray by false and deceptive beliefs. The effect on us and those we love is enormous. Paul warns us in his letter to the Colossians, "See to it that no one takes you captive through hollow and deceptive philosophy, which depends on human tradition and the basic principles of this world rather than on Christ." (Colossians 2:8) He warns Timothy, "Guard what has been entrusted to your care. Turn away from godless chatter and the opposing ideas of what is falsely called knowledge, which some have professed and in so doing have wandered from the faith." (I Tim. 6:20,21)

Why this philosophy is spiritually empty

Psychologists teach that our happiness is determined by our good self-esteem. That can happen only through our achievements and accomplishments. Our success is equal only to how much we believe in ourselves. If we can build up our self-esteem, then we can improve our accomplishments and our quality of life. In other words, love for ourselves is conditional. We must earn it and do what we think is valuable to deserve it. This sets up a vicious cycle in our thinking. We must have self-worth to achieve, but we must achieve to have self-worth. We must have self-esteem to have confidence, but we must be confident in order to feel self-esteem.

"I" am being held up by "Myself." This is nothing more than a spiritual house of cards that can come tumbling down at any moment. And when it does, "it it will fall with a great crash." (Matthew 7:27) Where is our refuge when we fail? Our abilities and feelings of self-worth fluctuate like a roller coaster.

How discouraging and frightening it is to live our lives based on this belief.

This shaky philosophy has penetrated our thinking of our everyday lives. What I do, what I buy, where I live, who I am married to, what my family accomplishes are goals to pursue in order to feed this bottomless pit called self-esteem. It can never be satisfied. I must continue to achieve and be competent to be happy. Where does it end?

Praise God that He has given us so much more than empty, human philosophy. He has given us His love freely. He has firmly planted us in His heart and our roots go deep down into His unchanging affection for us, His children. He has promised never to leave us or forsake us. He has promised to bless those who put their trust in Him rather than themselves.

2. How do we acquire self-esteem?

Both psychology and God's word teach us about our worth, and how to get it. Upon close comparison, though, we find some very opposing ideas. It is critical that we make these comparisons so that we can discern truth from error, and be safeguarded by truth. When we are, every aspect of our lives will be blessed.

The apostle Paul warns us about false teachers in I Timothy 6:20,21. "Timothy, guard what has been entrusted to your care. Turn away from godless chatter and the opposing ideas of what is falsely called knowledge." These words are just as true today as when Paul wrote them.

The teaching of good self-esteem is a counterfeit of the real worth God gives us. The purpose of a counterfeit is to deceive and to steal by substituting the counterfeit for the real thing. It is always harmful to the person who is deceived by it, whether it is counterfeit money or a counterfeit of God's truth. The counterfeit robs the person of the genuine. The way to recognize a counterfeit is to compare it with the genuine. Therefore we must ask two questions: What does God's word teach us that psychology doesn't, and how is psychology's idea harmful or deceptive? When we know the genuine, we will want to reject the counterfeit. We will discover that God's word is truth and we are blessed in countless ways when we live by it. Paul prayed for us to know the real from the counterfeit.

"I keep asking that the God of our Lord Jesus Christ, the glorious Father, may give you the Spirit of wisdom and revelation, so that you may know him better. I pray also that the eyes of your heart may be enlightened in order that you may know the hope to which he has called you, the riches of his glorious inheritance in the saints." (Ephesians 1:17-18)

We will consider four examples of the steps psychology says to take to acquire self-esteem and weigh each of them against scripture.

a. <u>Face your fears-they aren't as bad as you think they are. Facing your fears increases your confidence.</u>

The Bible has much to say about fear. All of us have fears because we are weak creatures. Every culture has fears of nature, danger, deprivation, pain, sickness, the future, and finally death itself. This statement that our fears are not as bad as we think is a denial of the realities of life. We are ignoring the trembling of our heart. Our fears are based on the fact that we are helpless creatures who have no power to control our world.

If I have to overcome my fears by my own wits, I am doomed to remain fearful, no matter how hard I try to talk myself out of it. These fears will have a negative influence on my life, if I do not turn to God.

God's word gives us hope. He gives us many promises regarding our fears. In Psalm 27:1 David says, "The Lord is my light and my salvation, Whom shall I fear? The Lord is the stronghold of my life. Of whom shall I be afraid?"

In Psalm 34:4, David is honest about his fears when he says, "I sought the Lord and he answered me; he delivered me from all my fears."

These verses show us that God is the only one who can take away our fears and give us confidence. That confidence is not in myself, but in the sovereign King of the Universe who has everything under His control. How wonderful. What strength and hope this means. What security and peace when I trust Him instead of myself.

The Bible tells us that there is one fear that we should have. It is a fear that we must not deny or ignore. It is a fear that opens the doorway of our heart to Him, and leads to life. It is the fear of the Lord. It is good, it is clean, it is pure. Proverbs 1:7 tells us that "the fear of the Lord is the beginning of wisdom." It is a mark of humility and worship. It is recognition of who He is, the sovereign holy Creator of the universe, and an admission of who I am, a sinful, helpless, needy creature. (Some would say that doesn't sound much like good self-esteem!)

Jesus gave us a good reason to fear God. In His blunt, "shoot from the hip" style, He says in Luke 12:5, "I tell you, my friends, do not be afraid of those who kill the body and after that can do no more. But I will show you whom you should fear: Fear him who, after the killing of the body, has power to throw you into hell."

C.S. Lewis captures this thought in the Chronicles of Narnia. Talking about Aslan, the lion King, he says, "This King is not safe, but He is good."

It is a paradox that we are to fear this holy God because He is all-powerful, but we are also to trust Him and His goodness for the very same reason- because He is all-powerful. In the same breath that He tells us to fear God, Jesus goes on to say, "Are not five sparrows sold for two pennies? Yet not one of them is forgotten by God. Don't be afraid. You are worth more than many sparrows" (Luke 12:6,7) Our fear of Him and our trust in Him are both based in His almighty power and control over the Universe.

It is one of the paradoxes in the Gospel that when we empty ourselves of our own self-worth, which the Bible calls pride, and realize that without Christ we are nothing, then we receive God's undeserved love, and we receive the precious worth He gives us.

Yes, God is the One who gives us true worth. He is the one who gives us genuine confidence- not in ourselves, but in Him. Once we have experienced the worth God gives by showing us His love, we realize that all the self-esteem we can muster does not compare.

b. "Forget your failures- learn from them. Avoid making the same mistakes again but don't limit yourself by assuming you failed before so you can't succeed this time. Try again- you're wiser and stronger. Don't be trapped in the past."

Again we are being told that in order for us to build our own self-esteem, we must "forget," i.e. "deny," and "pretend" something contrary to what we know to be true about ourselves. This thinking does not change us or our past, or lead to forgiveness for our failures.

This statement reiterates the idea that lack of self-worth comes from lack of success. To have self-worth, we must be successful and empowered by confidence. The only thing it can advise us to do is to try again......and again.........and again, only to fail again.......and again......and again. Deep down in our hearts, we know that forgetting our past can never erase the past. Our conscience condemns us. Nothing we do can ever remove the guilt for our past failures and sins, or change us to be a new person. Forgetting or compensating for our failures can never take away our shame and guilt.

Psychotherapists state that the number one problem in their patients is guilt, and there is no pill for that. Emotions of shame and guilt can be paralyzing. They can lead to such despondency as to make a person give up and lose the desire to live. As God's children, we need to believe what God says about failure and forgiveness, rather than buying into this worldly philosophy. He wants to make us whole, and that cannot happen if we believe in a counterfeit.

R.C. Sproul, of Ligonier Ministries, tells the story of of his psychiatrist friend, who offered R.C. a job. This friend was willing to pay R.C. a large annual salary to come and work for him. R.C. laughed and asked his friend why in the world he would want R.C. R.C. said to him, "I don't know anything about psychology or depression or anxiety or whatever. Why in the world would you make this offer to me?"

The friend said with utmost seriousness, "R.C. my patients don't need psychotherapy or medication. They need forgiveness from guilt. And you are the one that can show them the way to have that."

God's word resounds with hope and offers transformation. It does not rationalize away the truth of what we are, but speaks to the deepest longing of our heart- that is to be forgiven of sin, freed from its guilt, cleansed from its shame, and transformed to be the person we were created to be. It promises that we will be forgiven, changed, redeemed, and restored to God, our heavenly Father. He will give us new desires, new thoughts, new habits, new behavior. We will be born again.

The heart of God's heroine is set free and transformed into all that God created her to be.

What did God have to do to forgive us? What price had to be paid for our failures, our sins? The Bible answers, "Surely he took up our infirmities and carried our sorrows, yet we considered him stricken by God, smitten by him and afflicted. But he was pierced for our transgressions, he was crushed for our iniquities;

the punishment that brought us peace was upon him, and by his wounds we are healed." (Isaiah 53:4-6)

God loves us so much that He stopped at nothing to pay for the punishment our sins deserved and rescue us from an eternity without Him. By sending His son, Jesus, to pay for our salvation with His sinless body, and His perfect blood, He has given us unsurpassed worth. This worth is immeasurably more wonderful than any worth we could bestow on ourselves.

When something is being appraised for its worth, it is usually done in terms of the price that was paid for it. The higher the amount of money paid for it, the more worth it has. That is because the worth is measured in terms of the sacrifice the buyer is willing to make in return for the thing being bought. If it cost nothing to the buyer, it would have no worth. In the language of money that we can relate to, God tells us, "You are not your own. You were bought at a price." (I Corinthians 6:20) "It was not with perishable things such as silver or gold that you were redeemed from the empty way of life handed down to you from your forefathers, but with the precious blood of Christ, a lamb without blemish or defect." (I Peter 1:18,19)

What more worth could I desire than to know that God loved me so much that He would purchase me at such a great cost to Himself, for such a high price as Jesus' precious blood?

I do not have to forget my failures, or keep trying to succeed to have self-worth. I can rejoice, not in my ability to succeed, but in the truth that all my failures were paid for and that God has made me new.

Psalm 34:5 says, "Those who look to him are radiant; their faces are never covered with shame."

That sounds like a woman who knows her worth and value in God's eyes! Will you settle for a counterfeit?

c. Know what you want and ask for it. You deserve your dreams to come true.

Perhaps it seems unnecessary to analyze this statement. One may take it with a grain of salt, and deny that it is advocating a self-centered philosophy. It seems harmless enough to believe this. After all, what is wrong with asking for what I want and believing that I deserve my dreams to come true? Don't I deserve that?

This is another statement that is accepted in our culture. If we don't let scripture shape our thinking, we will reap the fruit of worldly philosophy. We will not be changed by God's Spirit and will not experience the joy of knowing Him deeply, and the fullness of His blessings.

As humans, we are made up of many layers. We experience many things that are not spiritual. We eat, work, play, and love. We have jobs, friends, hobbies, and recreation. We go to school, the mall, the hardware store, and the doctor. We drive to the gym, the bank, the post office and the cleaners. We go on vacation and visit family and celebrate holidays and birthdays. We cut our hair and kiss our baby's soft cheek and wash the dishes and drink hot tea with cookies. We laugh and cry and feel the joy of new life, the anguish of losing a loved one, and the sorrow of death. We relish the warm summer sunshine on our faces, and shiver at the freezing cold of winter on our cheeks. We are comforted by soft blankets, warm socks, affectionate hugs, and kind smiles. We are human.

But we are more than just these things. We need not look very deep into our soul to see that we also have self-centeredness, pride, a desire for our own glory, our own way, our own comforts, our own property, etc. We know we have bad moods, bad days, and bad attitudes. It is part of our nature to think more of ourselves than we do of others.

It is in this layer, our heart, that God speaks to us. His word tells us something very different than these statements about building our self-esteem. Let's compare these with the James 4:1-3. It sounds like James wrote it in direct answer to this viewpoint, even though he wrote it 2,000 years ago.

"What causes fights and quarrels among you? Don't they come from your desires that battle within you? You want something but don't get it. You kill and covet, but you cannot have what you want. You quarrel and fight. You do not have because you do not ask God. When you ask, you do not receive, because you ask with the wrong motives, so that you may spend what you get on your pleasures." (James 4:1-3)

Our problem is not that we need to get what we want, but that we want the wrong things. Our self-centered nature will never be satisfied. We will act and speak selfishly to get what we want, because of our sinful nature.

James' words profoundly refute this self-esteem statement, but God's word never leaves us stuck with our problem without providing the answer. James goes on to tell us how we should think, and what we should do. It assures us with the promise of what God will do when we obey. James 4:6-8,10 exclaims "God opposes the proud but gives grace to the humble. Submit yourselves, then, to God. Resist the Devil and he will flee from you. Come near to God and He will come near to you. Humble yourselves before the Lord, and He will lift you up."

God calls us to stop being superficial in our walk with Him. He urges us to take His word into the deepest part of our souls and be changed from our proud selfish selves into humble women who are like His Son. Nothing will do more to satisfy our hunger for happiness and fulfillment than receiving His grace, because He will lift us up.

d. Reward yourself when you succeed. No one else will! Isn't everything easier when you take time to help yourself?

Yourself....Yourself......Yourself.... By now, after examining the 3 other steps, we come back again to the central focus of the steps to building self-esteem. We have reiterated that our problem is self-centeredness and that Jesus died to set us free from our self-centered ways. We have seen from the scriptures that "myself," is my biggest obstacle to God's grace and that I must surrender my selfish heart to His Lordship. Let us look at this fourth statement in the light of scripture and see why it leads us away from the truth. God's word is faithful to speak to this issue.

This is, I think, perhaps the statement that is the most insulting to God's goodness. How I would like to cry out with righteous indignation,

"'No one else will!?' No one else will reward you? That is a lie. (Remember Satan's lie to Eve in chapter 5) The Bible promises in many places that God will reward those who are obedient to Him!"

Let's look at some verses that are filled with promise, that speak of rewards that are eternal and secure. And let's ask ourselves, "What cheap temporary reward could I possibly give to myself that could even compare to the eternal riches of God's grace and love, treasures in heaven where moth and rust do not destroy, and thieves do not break in and steal?' " (Matthew 6:20)

If we do a word study of the word "reward," we will be rewarded for our study. So get your concordance and look up reward (both nouns and verbs).

In Jeremiah 17:9,10 Jeremiah, the prophet, states a fact about the human heart and asks a question: "The heart is deceitful above all things and beyond cure. Who can understand it?"

The Lord answers him. "I the Lord search the heart and examine the mind to reward a man according to his conduct, according to what his deeds deserve."

Like we read in James 4, this verse from Jeremiah is in direct opposition to man's idea. We do not realize how deceitful our hearts are. We never judge ourselves correctly. Our idea of success is not God's idea. Our human appraisal of our goodness is nothing more than a vapor. God, on the other hand, searches our hearts perfectly with His laser beam of truth. We can be sure that He knows us better than we know ourselves. Yet, in spite of our imperfection, He will reward us according to our deeds, if our hearts belong to Him. Psalm 19:11 promises us, "In keeping [the Lord's commandments] there is great reward."

In Psalm 62:11, 12, David specifies two unshakeable truths he has learned. He says, "One thing God has spoken, two things have I heard; that you, O God, are strong, and that you, O Lord, are loving. Surely you will reward each person according to what he has done."

Jesus, may this be our testimony and legacy as we walk with you for the rest of our lives.

Take It To Heart:

"This is what the Lord says:
Let not the wise boast of their wisdom.
Let not the strong boast of their strength.
Let not the rich boast of their riches.
But let those who boast, boast about this:
That they have the understanding to know Me,
That I am the Lord, who exercises kindness,
Justice, and righteousness on earth,
For in these I delight, declares the Lord."
Jeremiah 9:23-24

Link to article, "A Short History of Self-esteem"
http://www.centreforconfidence.co.uk/pp/overview.php?p=c2lkPTYmdGlkPTAmaWQ9MTY0

CHAPTER 7

Amazing Love! How Can It Be?

"I have loved you with an everlasting love; I have Drawn you with you with unfailing kindness."
Jeremiah 31:3

A King and a Daughter

I have been experiencing God's amazing goodness for almost 50 years. It has been the most wonderful thing that has ever happened to me. I can say that the most exciting adventure in my Christian walk has been the changes He has done in me, my identity, my weaknesses, my old ways. This adventure is not visible or spectacular. It is sweet, quiet, and mysterious. God is so amazingly personal and gentle, compassionate and good. The longer I know Him, the more His word proves itself to be true. He has never failed to do what His word promises to me. But it has been a process. It did not happen overnight. Slowly but surely, He has worked in me, chipping away at the flaws, and molding His character in me. Each time He has brought about a change,

I have always seen that it was for my good. Every change He has done in me has given me hope and fulfilled a desire I hardly knew I had. Becoming like Him is the life of joy and peace. And yet I resisted Him for so long!

The Disney movie, Princess Diaries, is the story of the metamorphosis of Mia Thermopolis. A young, awkward teenager discovers that her father is a prince from another country, and that she is a princess by birth and a citizen of another kingdom. The story unfolds of the transformation of this young American girl into a gracious, elegant, princess. At first she did not want to change, but slowly, in her identity, she became a new young lady.

And this happened when she found out who her father was.

What a beautiful picture of what happens to each of us when we become God's child, a daughter of the King. Because He becomes our Father, we no longer have the same identity. We have new aspirations to live for Him instead of living for ourselves. We have a new heart that wants to live in obedience to God, out of a desire to please the One who loves us and died for us. We have a new a destiny, we are citizens of a new country. We have a new home where we will live someday-heaven. Our home is no longer this world with all its vain treasures. Our treasures are now in heaven with God. Our life now becomes a miracle because He gives us a new heart, the heart of a heroine.

Extreme Makeover

Like Mia Thermopolis, we change by a slow process. It doesn't happen overnight just because we believe in Christ. God transforms us by renewing our mind (Romans 12:2) He works in us to will and to act according to His good purpose. (Philippians 2:13) And He promises that He who has begun this good work in you will continue until it is completed., and you are with Christ. (Philippians 1:6) The process of change will continue until we get to heaven. And it is done by His power, not our own.

This process is the subject of this book. All of us who love Jesus have a godly desire to be changed. We want to behave the way God tells us to; we want to obey what we read in Scripture. However, often we see ourselves failing, and we struggle against our sin and weaknesses, and we become discouraged. It seems that there are so many obstacles in our way that we will never reach the goal. We realize that becoming more like Christ is similar to an extreme makeover. However, it is not as simple a process as changing my hair color, losing a few pounds, getting a facelift, and wearing new styles of clothes. No. It is much more than that. It is a process of changing my will, losing myself, getting a heart lift, and wearing the new nature, which is like Jesus. It is exchanging guilt for forgiveness, pride for humility, bitterness for contentment, fear for faith, anxiety for peace, heartache for comfort, disillusionment for hope, and sorrow for joy. Now that is an extreme makeover! What joy! What hope! There is nothing in this life to compare.

God changes us through the power of His love working in our hearts. He does not demand that we change ourselves and reject us until we do. He does not say that He will love us only when we are good and we deserve His love. He does not change us by ridiculing us or condemning us No. When we come to Him through Jesus, His amazing love heals our broken heart, whether our heart was broken by our own sin, by tragedy and heartache, or by another person's sin against us. He changes us on the inside, in our will, so that we want to act and live differently from our old life. "It is God who works in you to will and to act according to His good purpose." (Philippians 2:13) We now want to obey Him. All our love for Him and obedience to Him is our response to the fact that He first loved us. "This is love-not that we loved God, but that He loved us and sent His Son as an atoning sacrifice for our sins." (I John 4:10)

Knowing our Father

In order to be changed by God's amazing love, we must learn and believe what the Bible tells us about Him and His love. His word is the documented proof of His message to us. His word is the source of our faith. "Faith comes from hearing the message, and the message is heard through the word of Christ." (Romans 10:17) My faith cannot grow and be strengthened without knowing His word. He reveals his attributes and character to us through His word. As we discover who He is, we change to become more like Him. "We are being transformed into His likeness with ever-increasing glory." (II Corinthians 3:18) This is a self-improvement program like none other. In fact it is not a self-improvement program at all. It is a new birth, a new life. It is the paradox of the Gospel that I change, not when I try to change myself, but when I change in my understanding of God.

A.W. Tozer says in his book, Knowledge of the Holy, "No religion has ever been greater than its idea of God (even Christianity). The most significant fact about any man is not what he at a given time may say or do, but what he in his deep heart conceives God to be like." Knowing and believing God transforms our thinking and character.

God wants to have an intimate relationship with His children. He knows that a child cannot draw near to someone he doesn't trust and love. We cannot draw near to God if we do not know what He is like and how He loves us thoroughly, purely, perfectly, and tenderly.

Amazing Love

God's love is greater than my mind can conceive. It stretches beyond the horizons of my scrawny, finite imagination. It defies reason, contradicts logic, and "surpasses knowledge." To say that it is wonderful is not enough. I must believe that it is more wonderful than my mind can imagine. "No eye has seen, no ear has heard, no mind has conceived what God has prepared for those who love Him." (I Corinthians 2:9) I must believe that its perfection is purer and holier than I can ever know or understand. It is this admission of the fact that I cannot comprehend it that sets me free to accept my intellectual limitations and rejoice that such things are too wonderful to understand.

A soaring eagle ascends beyond the clouds, lifted by its mighty wings into a majestic blue sky, to which my earthbound limbs can never carry me. As the magnificent creature disappears from sight, my thoughts do not fall back to earth like a deflated balloon; rather, they compel me to realize that the eagle has entered a realm beyond my vision and understanding. It bids me to contemplate that which is beyond my grasp and be filled with wonder and awe. Like the eagle's flight, the words we use to describe God's love lift our thoughts higher, where they lead us to the limits of our understanding and then invite us to see that there is infinitely more beyond. The love of God is higher and deeper and wider and longer than time and space, than eternity itself. Paul prayed that believers " being rooted and established in love, may have power to grasp how wide and long and high and deep is the love of Christ, and to know this love that surpasses knowledge." (Eph.3:18,19)

Human Love Is Not Like God's Love

Any love we have ever received from another human being, or have ever been able to give to another person, cannot give us a glimpse into the perfect, infinite love of God for us. Our human idea of love is absurdly inferior to what God's love is, and no comparison between the two would even be reasonable.

As human beings, we are able to love only in a limited way. I may love someone deeply, but because of my selfishness I lack the power to love as I ought. My sins of anger, resentment, jealousy, self-pity, impatience, to name a few, all show me that it is impossible for me to love others as God loves me. My ability to love is only equal to my character, and consistent with my nature. I am imperfect, so my love is imperfect. I find my selfish human nature in conflict with my claims to truly love another person. Add to this the fact that all human beings are unable to love as God does. I have never loved anyone and no one has ever loved me the way God does.

God, on the other hand, is perfect, pure, holy, all-powerful, all-knowing, and all truth. His love is equal to his nature, and an expression of His holy, perfect character. His attributes never contradict or restrict His boundless love. He loves us because His heart is consumed with our welfare and our well-being. Like a mother with a new infant, He thinks of nothing else. Night and day He thinks of us- our needs and our safety. He knows our joys, our pains, our fears, and our destiny. He is never distracted or bored with us. His compassion for our needs does not cool because He becomes tired. He never lacks the resources to meet those needs. His delight in us does not fade because He is busy or annoyed. He is engrossed in caring for every little detail of our lives. Because He is perfect and righteous, His infatuation with us is not perverted by wrong motives. His love is not that of a possessive husband who desires to control for his own fulfillment;. His infatuation with us is not that of an emotional teenager whose affections flit from one love to another depending on the moment. His jealousy does not imprison us or deprive us of our fulfillment and happiness, but seeks our highest good. He will fiercely protect us from any threat to that good, even if that threat comes from ourselves through our own rebellion and sin. His tenderness never causes Him to make unwise or biased judgments. He is not like a doting, sentimental father, who is blind to the manipulative charms of his favorite child.

God's perfect, pure, unchanging, all-knowing, all consuming love for us cannot possibly contain anything evil, harmful, wrong, or unwise. His complete knowledge of us means that nothing in us is hidden from Him. His passion for us causes His will for us to be always good. His desire for us causes Him to take pleasure in us, and His affection for us causes Him to delight in giving Himself sacrificially to us. Like a mother's milk flows continually to her nursing child, God's love flows from His heart without measure. There is never less than when we started, it is never consumed or spent. We don't have to wait for the supply to be refilled, or rationed out to us in measly portions. We don't have to convince, persuade, or beg. We don't have to wait in line or compete with His other children for His love and attention. There need be no sibling rivalry among God's children. And God does not neglect a single one of His children for even a fraction of a second.

Believing What God Says About Himself

In spite of the greatness of God's love, we often relate to Him as though we don't believe that this love is gracious, free, and amazing. Our incomplete knowledge of God hinders our faith and our relationship with Him. We know some characteristics about God, but often one of those characteristics seems to oppose another. Take for example, His justice and His mercy. I have found that I cannot understand how both attributes can be equally true simultaneously. I cannot believe that God will forgive me when His justice tells me that I deserve punishment. At other times, I cannot believe He is able or willing to answer my prayer. I may believe that God loves me, but because I don't know that He is in control of everything, I cannot trust He is able carry it out. I may believe that God is all-powerful, but I question whether or not He will use His power to work on my behalf.

Our incomplete and faulty understanding of God hinders us from trusting Him and prevents us from approaching Him when we most need Him. In our sins, our conscience condemns us. Our needs and failures cause us to see only those things that make us afraid to come to Him. We fear his judgment and punishment. We are afraid His words will be a harsh and heavy burden, giving us more sorrow than comfort. In contrast, I John 4:18 tells us that "perfect love drives out fear." In this verse, God is calling to us to trust in His love and not hide from Him when we need Him more than ever.

When we learn what God reveals about Himself in His word, and trust in His perfection, then we find that each of His attributes supports and upholds the others. We realize that if our God were all-loving but not all-powerful, He would be unable to provide all that He desires to give. If He were all-powerful but not all-loving, He would have the ability to meet our every need, but would not be moved with compassion to do so. If He were all-loving but not all-knowing, then He would be unable to love everything about us because so much of ourselves would be hidden from Him. If He were all-knowing but not all-loving, His knowledge would bring judgment and condemnation, rather than mercy and forgiveness. Oh yes, and we could go on and on as we gaze into the exquisite facets of this Holy God, each facet working together with all the others, so that there is no contradiction, no inconsistency, no favoritism, no fickleness. There is only perfection. Our God is perfectly wise, perfectly trustworthy, perfectly wonderful.

When we know of God's character as revealed in His word, then we can trust in His love. It is only as we respond to His love by letting Him change us that we will be whole and our soul will be satisfied.

The Joyful Life

We desperately need to let God's love fill our hearts and heal our souls. We are fainting spiritually but we don't know what to do. We think there is something more that we must do to put our lives back together or fix our situations. All the while, it is knowing God's love that enables us to trust Him. We are amazed at this wonderful God- a Being that is so high above our understanding that we cannot comprehend Him, and yet a God so kind as to take on human flesh, to be like us so that we could know Him and have a relationship with Him. When we think about the God of the Bible, we can only feel awe and humility. He is the only one who loves us with the perfect love that meets our deepest needs and transforms our heart into the heart of His heroine.

Take It To Heart:

"For I am convinced that neither death nor life, neither angels nor demons, neither the present nor the future, nor any powers, neither height nor depth, nor anything else in all creation, will be able to separate us from the love of God that is in Christ Jesus our Lord."

Romans 8:38,39

CHAPTER 8

Bridal Trousseau

"As a bridegroom rejoices over his bride,
So will your God rejoice over you."
Isaiah 62:5b

Not Of This World

God's plan is wonderful, paradoxical, and mysterious, and impossible to explain. This transformation begins when we lose our old life and receive His new life. Jesus says in Matthew 16:25, "Whoever wants to save his life will lose it, but whoever loses his life for me will find it." How do we understand this paradox? How can we make sense of such a thought-if I lose my life for His sake I will find it? Doesn't this contradict everything I have always believed and every choice I have ever made for myself? Doesn't this sound ludicrous in the midst of the voices that continually tell me to look out for myself, indulge myself, reward myself? You bet it does. It sounds ludicrous, unrealistic, naïve, and even impractical. Jesus' words shake the foundations of our thinking, like an earthquake that rumbles through rock and ground, unsettling everything in its path. He turned man's thinking upside down.

The entrance of the Son of God to this world was an earthquake of love. It was an explosion of hope. It rattled the gates of hell, and demolished its very foundation. It destroyed the power of Satan. It annihilated DEATH.

And it set us free.

It freed us from our old lives and our old ways. It provided the way for us to have a new heart and all that that includes- our character, our mind, our identity, our soul, and our self. We are a new creation in every way. Godliness will restructure a woman's priorities, goals, careers, and reputations. As women of God, we will impact our world, and transform families, communities, and churches.

When we receive Christ into our hearts by believing the Gospel-that His death personally paid for our sins-we enter into a whole new world with different rules and ways of doing things. We live in a new kingdom, of which the risen Christ is the perfect King. We serve a new Ruler, who gives His servants new hearts, with new attitudes and desires. He gives us a new nature. Just as it is human nature to be selfish, it is Christ's nature to be unselfish. It is human nature to be proud. It is our Master's dear nature to be humble. It is human nature to be self-centered. It was Jesus' nature to be God-centered for He said, "I do nothing on my own but speak just what the Father has taught me. The one who sent me is with me; He has not left me alone, for I always do what pleases Him." (John 8:28,29) He said to the crowds, "..I am from above. You are of this world; I am not of this world." (John 8:23)

As His servants, His heroines, we have a new center, and that center is Christ. We have a new heart-the engine that generates our motives, and drives our thoughts, goals, plans, and desires. Our identity now comes from identifying with our Savior. We want to be like Him. We have a new Master, not our "self," not our "will," but Christ. We lose our life so that we can find it. We give up our right to seek our own way to happiness, and in the process we find the only true happiness there is-the happiness that is genuine, eternal and free. Just as our self-concept developed when we were first born, now a new identity develops in our new nature. Now, because Jesus lives in us through His indwelling Holy Spirit, it is He that we want to obey.

And this is a great mystery.

The Great Mystery

It is a mystery because we can only believe it by faith.

It is a mystery because it cannot be understood with the natural mind.

This mystery is the Gospel-which was hidden before Christ came to this earth.

If you believe in Christ, He is living inside you. You are now a godly woman.

"The mystery of godliness is great." (I Tim.3:16)

Isn't that wonderful? Does it fill your heart with excitement to think that you are a miracle and your life is involved in a mystery? That you have had a mystery revealed to you because God has had mercy on you? That you have received something more glorious than words can express, that the world can never understand or give?

The apostle Paul thought so, for he describes the gospel as the "glorious riches of this mystery, which is Christ in you, the hope of glory." (Colossians 1:27)

Extreme Makeover Begins

It is important to realize that becoming a Christian does not instantly change us so that we stop doing all the wrong things we did before we were saved. The Christian walk is a life-long journey of learning to be more and more obedient to God, and less and less obedient to my old self. As John the Baptist said in John 3:30, "He must become greater; I must become less."

When a woman is born again by faith, and Jesus lives inside her heart, He begins the process of changing her to become more like Him. As Christians, we need to understand what the Bible says about this process. Understanding this process will encourage us when we go through painful, difficult times, because the Bible teaches us that God has a purpose in our trials. When we can know the process He is taking us through, we can trust God more and surrender to His plan.

God is so good because He did not leave us in the dark about His process that works in us while we walk with Him on this journey called Life. The New Testament is our training manual. It tells us about the extreme makeover He is doing on us, and what we can expect as we go through it. Paul says it in a nutshell in Colossians 3:5, 9, 10, "Put to death, therefore, whatever belongs to your earthly nature. You have taken off your old self with its practices and have put on the new self, which is being renewed in knowledge in the image of its Creator." (Read the whole passage, verses 1-10, to know the context of what Paul is saying.)

The words "taken off" and "put on" are words that were used in the context of clothing ourselves. We take off an old coat, or put on a new dress. We take off our makeup and put on a new look with a new color of eyeshadow and a new shade of blush. (He must have known that we women could really relate to that terminology!) We are to put off our old self and clothe ourselves with Christ. We do this because we were created in His image. He is perfect, beautiful, without spot or blemish.

And He wants us to be like Him!

Jesus said that those who are His will "shine like the sun in the kingdom of their Father." (Matthew 13:43)

Now then, what is this process that we call extreme makeover? What can we expect? Well, let me put it this way – I have good news and bad news. The good news is that God is going to polish you up and make you shine and you will be new. The bad news is- it's going to hurt!

But listen! There is a reason!

The reason is because He loves you-so deeply, so completely.

And look! There is a promise!

The promise is that you will possess true joy and peace that you never could have had in your old life.

In the world of athletics and fitness, it is an accepted motto-"no pain, no gain." We should not be surprised when our muscles are sore and our bodies fatigued. When we begin a new training program at the gym, we are always encouraged to know that our pain is a good sign that indicates that something of value is happening; it is a sign of improvement and progress toward the desired results.

In the same way, Peter tells us, "Do not be surprised at the painful trial you are suffering, as though something strange were happening to you." (I Peter 4:12)

It is comforting to know that it is not strange to go through painful trials as a Christian. We can have hope in that thought. Let's see what the Bible says about why God brings trials into our lives.

The Bridal Trousseau

The Bible teaches that those who have a relationship with God through His son, Jesus, are the bride of Christ. Christ is the bridegroom. In the New Testament, in Israel, when a woman was betrothed to a man, she did not know when her wedding day would be. She had to wait and prepare herself for that wonderful day. And she had to be ready when her beloved bridegroom arrived. When the wedding day dawned, the bridegroom would begin his journey to his bride's home to take his beloved away from her old home and take her to her new one after the marriage ceremony. In the same way, Jesus is going to come back to earth to take us to heaven, where we will live the only real "And they lived happily ever after" love story that has ever happened, or ever could happen. We have His promise, for He says in John 14:1-3, "Do not let your hearts be troubled. Trust in God; trust also in me. In my Father's house are many rooms; if it were not so I would have told you. I am going there to prepare a place for you. And if I go and prepare a place for you, I will come back and take you to be with me that you also may be where I am."

During the months before her wedding, a Jewish bride made her trousseau-her new clothes for her new life. Her trousseau was cared for and put away to protect it from stain or wrinkle, so that it would be spotless and perfect as she began her new life with her husband. As the bride of Christ we also have received a new trousseau. We are to wear Christ by clothing ourselves "with compassion, kindness, humility, gentleness, patience." (Colossians 3:12) As He works in us, we learn how to wear our new trousseau.

Usually when a bride goes to a dressmaker to have her trousseau made to fit her, the dressmaker takes her measurements. The dressmaker cuts and sews the garment and fits it onto the bride. She tucks and pins, trims and gathers, and makes it smaller or larger until it is shaped to fit perfectly. As the bride of Christ, we have our garments made to fit by a different process. Instead of altering the garment to fit us, God alters us to fit the garments! Ouch! Can you imagine if your body were cut and pinned and stitched to fit a dress, rather than the other way around? (I would find a new dressmaker!)

Imagine, though, that you went to the dressmaker's shop and hanging there, on display, was the most exquisitely lovely gown you had ever seen. It was perfect in every way, and only a perfect figure could fit into it. How glad you would be if that dressmaker could change your figure to be the perfect size, to look breathtakingly beautiful for your beloved bridegroom on your glorious wedding day.

That is how God works in us. He has planned for us to put on His character, so He changes us, molds us, and fashions us to fit the beautiful garments of His Son, the robes of Jesus' righteousness. He pricks our conscience with the piercing straight pins of His word. He pulls and yanks on our will until we surrender to Him. He gathers His arms around our hearts with His Holy Spirit to comfort us in our trials. He wraps His love around us to give us hope that we belong to Him and are becoming like Him. He drapes His robes of righteousness over us and makes us exactly like Jesus.

God is making us holy, for that glorious wedding day, for we are His bride.

<u>"Christ loved the church and gave himself up for her to make her holy and to present her to Himself as a radiant church, without stain or wrinkle or any other blemish, but holy and blameless</u> (Ephesians 5:25- 27)

<u>The Purpose of our trials</u>

The purpose of the trials in our lives is to make us fit to wear these new garments. Our trials come in many forms, but they all are sent by the Lord to accomplish His purpose in us. That purpose is for us to become like Jesus.

Romans 8:28 says, <u>"In all things God works for the good of those who love Him, who have been called according to His purpose. For those God foreknew, he also predestined to be conformed to the likeness of His Son, that he might be the firstborn among many brothers</u> (and sisters, and that's you and me!).

The writers of the New Testament give us the reasons why God puts us through trials. They teach us the purpose of our pain and suffering and what God wants to accomplish through them.

<u>Romans 5:2-5:</u> We rejoice in the hope of the glory of God. Not only so but we also rejoice in our sufferings, because we know that suffering produces perseverance; perseverance, character; and character, hope. And hope does not disappoint us, because God has poured out His love into our hearts by the Holy Spirit, whom he has given to us.

II Corinthians 1:3-4: Praise be to the God and Father of our Lord Jesus Christ, the Father of compassion and the God of all comfort, who comforts us in all our troubles, so that we can comfort those in any trouble with the comfort we ourselves have received from God.

II Corinthians 1:8,9: We do not want you to be uninformed about the hardships we suffered. In our hearts we felt the sentence of death. But this happened that we might not rely on ourselves but on God.

Hebrews 12:7, 10, 11: Endure hardship as discipline; God is treating you as sons. For what son is not disciplined by his father? God disciplines us for our good, that we may share in his holiness. No discipline seems pleasant at the time but painful. Later on, however it produces a harvest of righteousness and peace for those who have been trained by it.

James 1:2-4, 12: Consider it pure joy, my brothers, whenever you face trials of many kinds, because you know that the testing of your faith develops perseverance. Perseverance must finish its work so that you may be mature and complete, not lacking anything. Blessed is the man, who perseveres under trial, because when he has stood the test, he will receive the crown of life that God has promised to those who love Him.

I Peter 1:6, 7: For a little while you may have had to suffer grief in all kinds of trials. These have come so that your faith- of greater worth than gold, which perishes, even though refined by fire- may be proved genuine and may result in praise, glory, and honor when Jesus Christ is revealed.

I Peter 4: 1, 2, 12, 13: Therefore, since Christ suffered in his body, arm yourselves with the same attitude, because he who has suffered in his body is done with sin. As a result he does not live the rest of his earthly life for evil human desires, but rather for the will of God. Dear friends, do not be surprised at the painful trial you are suffering, as though something strange were happening to you. But rejoice that you participate in the sufferings of Christ so that you may be overjoyed when his glory is revealed.

A Lesson From the Ants

One summer when my children were little, we were having an invasion of ants in the hot Temecula Valley. On this particular day, I watched a phenomenon I had never seen before.

In a large storage close, the shelves were full of books, boxes, photos, vacuum cleaner parts, trophies, extra light bulbs, and whatever else you can think of. At this time, because the children were little, we also had baskets and bins of toys, crayons, itty bitty doll shoes and dresses, cars and trucks, hackey sacks, and hockey pucks. We called this closet the supply room!

One day, however, something very curious was happening in the supply room. As I walked down the hall, I noticed a strange, thread-like black line along the wall about 12 inches above the floor. The line extended from the doorway of the supply room all the way to the doorway of my daughters' room. As I got a closer look, I was amazed to find that this thread-like line was an unbroken line of marching ants. I followed the line to its source. Coming in at the window of my daughters' room, these tiny soldiers, as if sent on a mission, threaded their way, single file, down the wall across the carpet, and up the doorway, where they entered the supply room. Continuing on relentlessly, they wound their way around every obstacle in their path, between boxes and baskets, finally coming to a little container of cheap toys from an arcade machine. There the march ended. I was strangely fascinated to see what I would find.

When I began my search, I was struck with the question, "What can they be looking for? What could possibly be attracting them? If this were happening in the kitchen, it would be understandable, but why the toy basket?"

Coming to the end of the line, my question was answered. I picked up the container and began to dig through the contents. "Why would ants want crayons and broken bits of plastic? I dug through and there, at the bottom of this pile of a child's collection of foolish treasures, I pulled out a shriveled wrapper with fragments of candy left inside and forgotten by one of my children long ago.

As I looked at the crumbled pieces in my hand, I learned something about our trials. The Lord made me think about how we deal with them, and try to avoid them. When we have ants, we want to get rid of them. We set out traps, or wipe them away with sprays, or call pest control. We consider them a nuisance. We think they are the problem. But that day, this tiny band of inspectors led me to something that needed to be cleaned out and thrown away. Without this highly organized miniature squadron, marching on- focused and commissioned- I would never have known this candy was hidden there in the closet.

Like the ants, God orchestrates and directs our trials, sometimes seemingly insignificant, but annoying and intruding, and sends them into our lives on His schedule. Other times our trials are larger. Large or small, our trials are directed, focused, and aimed at one thing- to reveal to us the things that God wants to throw away. He wants to clean out the boxes and throw away the useless counterfeits, so that He can give us the genuine good things that come from Him. And like the ants, God sends numerous trials that are similar. They repeat themselves- the same old conflicts, the same old fears, the same old failures. But these repetitious troubles are God's way of showing us what He wants to change, and what He is doing in us-making us like Jesus.

We were created in Christ to be like Him!

God's will is for us to see the trials in our lives as coming from Him for a purpose. When we surrender to His correction and admit the sins He is revealing to us through our trials, He changes us by His grace working in us. When we see our old selfish ways sloughing off, and our hearts wanting to do His will, then we know that we are experiencing His grace, and our hearts overflow with joy.

God's Precious Promise

Romans 8:28, 29 is God's promise to us that our trials will be used by God for our good. As we respond by believing that God wants to use these trials to change us, He promises to make us more like Jesus. Becoming like our Savior is the blessed, abundant life that Jesus declared He came to give us. (John 10:10)

This life is our reward and our joy, our wealth and our glorious inheritance. It is His grace and power flowing through our being, like the blood pulsing through our veins. It is redemption becoming a reality, forgiveness doing its work. It is the resurrected Christ living His life through His people. It is the Christian's very breath, food, and drink, because it results in knowing the Son of God, so that we "become mature, attaining to the whole measure of the fullness of Christ." (Ephesians 4:13)

It was this promise that made the great apostle Paul declare "For to me, to live is Christ (Philippians 1:21) I want to know Christ and the power of His resurrection and the fellowship of sharing in His suffering, becoming like Him in His death and so,somehow, to attain to the resurrection from the dead. (Philippians 3:10)

Take It To Heart:

"Therefore, I urge you, brothers and sisters, in view of God's mercy, to offer your bodies as living sacrifices, holy and pleasing to God-this is your true and proper worship. Do not conform to the pattern of this world, but be transformed by the renewing of your mind."

Romans 12:1,2

CHAPTER 9

Wandering In My Will-Derness

"The terrible thing, the almost intolerable thing, is to hand over your whole self - all your wishes and precautions - to Christ."
"Mere Christianity," C. S. Lewis

Dear Sister in Christ,

I would like to start off this chapter by thanking you for reading this far. I pray that the Lord has been speaking to you, comforting you, and encouraging you. Christ is the lover of our souls, and as a lover, He woos us to enter into a deeper experience of His love. He holds out His hand to us, and as we put our hand in His, He gently draws us closer to His heart. He proves to us that we can trust Him with every detail of our lives, along with all of our emotions, hurts, dreams, and desires. We can tell Him anything that we think, feel, or do without fear of mockery, condemnation, or betrayal. Because He became a man, we know we are talking to a person like ourselves. He calls Himself our brother and our friend. He loves us with the tenderness of a mother's heart, filled with a compassion that we cannot fathom..

So far we have contemplated many things that point us to our walk with God. We have discussed our identity-that powerful force within our hearts that drives us to find love, acceptance, security, and happiness. And we have taken a long, hard look at why our identity has kept us from God, what harm it is doing to us if we continue to live our lives using the same old methods that we always have. We have learned from His word what He wants to do in us, as He writes His story through us, His heroines. He is teaching us why He wants to change us, and the process He uses to accomplish that change.

Surrendering Our Will

As we begin this chapter, I feel it is important to share that this chapter is the seed from which this book grew. It is the story of what God has done in my life and I want to share with you how He set me free from my prison.

I had been a Christian for about ten years. I loved the Lord and His word, and wanted to live my life for Him. I perceived myself as obedient to the Lord because I wanted to do His will. I did not see myself as a strong-willed person because I never had been. I was an obedient child because of fear of my father, respect for the adults in my life, and a compliant personality. I was not stubborn or determined in getting my own way, not because of any virtue on my part, but because I didn't have the nerve. I did not have the confidence needed to insist on my own way. As a Christian I perceived myself in the same way. I had obeyed my parents, my teachers, school rules, and the law. I was an expert at obeying rules. I obeyed library rules, parking lot rules, laundromat rules, and cafeteria rules. You name it. I obeyed it! So when I found out that God wanted me to obey Him, I did not question it, or doubt that I was willing. What I found out was that God saw me differently. He knew He had work to do! (As the saying goes, "I was a piece of work!")

He chose to speak to me through my husband. I do not remember the details of this particular trial. The fact is that I was struggling in my life with a miserable, self-piteous attitude, which impelled me to act in a very ugly way. I didn't need to say or do anything. My black heart filled the house with its sour atmosphere, and chilled the rooms with bitter cold. My silence darkened every conversation, and shut down every spark of joy or laughter in my husband and little boys. I had always struggled with this problem when I was hurt or angry. I had learned to retreat into a protective fortress of stubborn silence. Little did I realize that this fortress was in actuality a concrete cell of solitary confinement. I did not care, as long as it kept others from hurting me more. What I did not realize was how much I was hurting those precious ones whom I loved.

It was time for the Lord to show me that it was a fault He wanted to change, a sin of which He wanted me to repent. My husband, who is the most wonderful Christian I know, with the great trepidation that a husband only feels when he is treading on a woman's dark mood, took the risk of pointing out to me how much my bitterness was hurting every member of the family. I recognized the truth of what he was saying but did not know what to do about it. I thought I wanted to repent and change but felt powerless. I thought that such a deep-seated change was impossible.

When he told me how he felt, I said, "I want to change but I just feel that I am too weak." (After all, I had always seen myself as compliant, which to me meant weak.)

His voice was gentle but direct. He answered, "Honey, I'm sorry, but I beg to differ with you. I think you are being very strong."

His words sliced through the air like a surgeon's gleaming, ice-cold scalpel. The Great Surgeon made the clean incision in my heart, and convicted me of a fact to which I had been blind all of my life. At that moment I experienced what Hebrews 4:12,13 declares.

"The word of God is living and active, sharper than any two-edged sword." It penetrated my heart, "dividing soul and spirit, joints and marrow." He had judged the "thoughts and attitudes of my heart, for nothing in all of creation is hidden from God's sight. Everything is uncovered and laid bare before the eyes of Him to whom we must give account." (Hebrews 4:12,13) I knew that God meant business.

That night I had a dream. I dreamt I was riding a horse. (I did not know the first thing about horseback riding.) It was a magnificent white steed. This horse was very hard to handle. I had to pull so hard on the reins I feared my arms weren't strong enough. I remember feeling how tough and strong this horse's neck was. The powerful muscles of his neck were arched in resistance to my control. It was single-minded and unyielding. I had never attempted to bring any force so strong as this under my control. My heart trembled in fear at the thought of where this wild beast would take me if I could not bring it under control. I cried out in my dream, "I can't control this horse!"

When I woke, the image that was strongly impressed on me was the tough, arched, resisting, powerfully strong neck of this beautiful white horse. This impression is as clear to me today as it was forty -five years ago.

The Lord spoke to my heart, "This horse is your will."

Five short words- quick and to the point! Those five words changed my life, but not without a long struggle of many years.

The outcome of this struggle has given me new freedom, peace, and joy. God wrestled with me, and conquered my will with His love. To show me the work He had done in my life, God gave me a sequel to this dream, about fifteen years after the first one. In this dream, I was riding a beautiful white steed, but this time it was decorated in fine-looking regalia. We were marching in a parade, and this horse's head was lifted up regally, his neck was gracefully relaxed in submission to the reins, which I held loosely in my hands. The horse's hooves lifted up off the ground in prancing steps, moving to the rhythm of the victorious music. I was exhilarated by the feeling of sitting atop this glorious creature that would now carry me safely and elegantly through the crowd.

It was a short but vivid dream (probably in color!). When I woke, God did not speak to me as He had the first time. He revealed to me that He was in the process of taming my stubborn, unbending will. A tamed will in the hands of her Creator is like a horse that is trusted enough to be ridden by her King in a parade! What a wonderful God we have!

It is for this reason that I write this book. I believe that, as Christian women, we need to face the fact that the hardest thing to surrender to God is our will, but surrendering our will to Him is the doorway to all that we desire and need. He wants to do more than we could ever ask or think, but He knows that our obstinate will is the barrier to His blessings.

Although God has done a miracle in my life, which He showed me in my dream, I still must surrender my will to Him daily. But, like a trained horse, as long as I am following the Lord's reins, and obeying His direction, my will is under control, and I have His peace reigning in my soul. We will never be free of our sinful nature on this earth, but we have hope that He is changing us from glory to glory. As we do, we know our God in a real life relationship. And that is our greatest joy

Strong Willed? Who? Me?

There is no possession more treasured, no property more protected, no battlefield more defended than my will. It is impossible to comprehend how surrendering my rights,my wishes, my abilities, and my goals to someone else could bring me more joy and happiness than my own plans can. It is impossible to believe that my wishes for myself may not be the most beneficial for me or in my best interest. Myself and my happiness are synonymous in my mind. How could they not be? I trust no one more than my own will to make the best decisions regarding my life. No one cares more about my needs or happiness than I. How can it happen that my will, the guardian and champion of Myself would turn out to be untrustworthy, incapable of thinking rightly on my behalf, a traitor to my cause, and the thief of true peace and joy. How can I be an enemy of myself?

The answer is found in God's word. My soul was created in God's image to have fellowship with Him. Because of sin, and separation from God, my will decides how I will govern myself, and plan my life with one end in mind-my happiness.

In Chapter 5, we read of how Satan tempted Eve. As Martin Luther puts it in his book, The Bondage of the Will, Satan "found the hinge on which all turns, and aimed for the vital spot." If he could make her want to disobey God, her will would forever come between her and her Creator. It would forever make her want to choose her own way rather than God's. And the result would be death. Because of Eve's sin to live independently of God, our will was born to live and choose and think and plan apart from any dependence on God, apart from wanting God's will. It is in competition with God for control of our life and our destiny. The Bible says our will is an enemy of God and hates God. It does not want to bow to any other lord or give up its position on the throne of our heart. Our soul is at the mercy of our tyrannical will which keeps us from wanting all the good that God desires for us, because surrender means its own defeat.

Paul explains in Romans 8:6-8 tells us, <u>"The mind of sinful man is death, but the mind controlled by the Spirit is life and peace; the sinful mind is hostile to God. It does not submit to God's law, nor can it do so. Those controlled by the sinful nature cannot please God."</u>

God is the lover of your soul. If you have received His Son, He has redeemed your life and has raised His banner in your heart, triumphing over every enemy, and claiming you as His own particular treasure. He has come to rescue you from the power of sin, and He has set you free from the tyrant that has ruled you and rebelled against His love and goodness.

Romans 6:17,18 assures us. "Thanks be to God that, though you used to be slaves to sin, you have been set free from sin have become slaves to righteousness."

Because of His great love for you and me He desires to conquer our will, which opposes His love and lordship when it wants to be in control. Oh that we would be willing to be set free from this slavery to such a master that opposes this amazing, loving God.

The Problem of My Will

Charles Dickens illustrates the power of our will in his tale, "A Christmas Carol." The first chapter begins with a dialogue between Scrooge and his business partner, Marley. Marley had died suddenly and his ghost appeared to Scrooge. Marley had lived by the same philosophies that drove Scrooge. Now that he could view his life from an eternal perspective, he came back to warn Scrooge of the folly of his life's choices. When Scrooge sees his friend's ghostly form, he notices that he is bound by a heavy chain, so he asks his friend,

"You are bound in this heavy chain. Tell me why."

Marley answers in a somber voice: "I wear the chain I forged in life. I made it link-by-link, yard-by-yard. I shackled myself of my own free will and of my own free will I wore it."

Then he asks Scrooge the penetrating question we must all ask ourselves, "Do you know the weight and length of the strong coil you bear yourself. It is a burdensome chain."

And I can say with Marley, " this chain, which my will, has bound around my soul, is oppressive, and burdensome."

The Bible's View of Man's Will

Paul warns us in his letter to the Galatians 6:7, "Do not be deceived. God cannot be mocked. A man reaps what he sows. The one who sows to please his sinful nature, from that nature will reap destruction. The one who sows to please (God's) Spirit, from the Spirit will reap eternal life.

In his letter to the Romans, he writes, "Don't you know that when you offer yourselves to someone to obey him as slaves, you are slaves to the one whom you obey, whether you are slaves to sin, which leads to death, or to obedience which leads to righteousness. You have been set free from sin and have become slaves to righteousness." (Romans 6:16,18)

This truth is in direct contrast to the contemporary view that man is basically good and is shaped by his environment. (See chapter 3.) For our soul's sake, we must understand why the bible's teaching is the truth and why it frees us. On the one hand, psychology says that we are a product of all the experiences we have had, and the environment we grew up in. There is a stigma attached to the idea that my will is my problem. We have an "I can't help it" mentality. (I mentioned at the beginning of this chapter that God had to show me this about myself.) The problem with that is that we see ourselves as victims, unable to change unless we can change our environment or our past. Since this is impossible, we are left with feelings of hopelessness. God's word, on the other hand convicts us of our sinful nature and rebellious will. He promises that when we take responsibility for our own choices and reactions to life, and surrender our will to Him, then we are set free from the past and our own nature. No one can keep us in bondage when Jesus sets us free. (John 8:6)

My Will and Self-Protection

In chapter 3, we learned how our self-concept develops. We learned that as we grow, we are constantly learning how to "take care of ourselves" in this dangerous, unkind world. We experience moments of happiness, sadness, pain, love, rejection, disappointment, and fulfillment. Through it all, we are learning the rules of the game in which each of us is a participant. We learn what we must do to be happy, safe, secure, and loved. We learn what works and what doesn't, what succeeds and what fails. We learn to hang on to the methods that work, and discard the ones that don't.

One of the strongest drives we have is self-protection. It is a God-given drive for survival. We learn very early in life that we don't like to be hurt in any way. We learn to protect ourselves by fleeing or fighting, depending on our personality.

A timid personality will shrink from hurt and pain, hoping that by avoiding it, she will be safe. A strong woman will face it head-on, because she knows that avoidance makes her more vulnerable, like a rabbit hiding in a hole. She has great inner strength and natural resources that she draws upon to protect herself, and fight for her rights. A beautiful person learns to protect her vulnerable heart by making the outside look good, hoping that the outside will compensate for the pain she feels on the inside. If it doesn't, at least it will hide her pain from the watching world. A perfectionist creates a perfect world for herself, where she can be in control of her environment and prevent pain and trouble from entering.

In the attempt to build a safe place to shield ourselves from pain, rejection and heartache, each of us finds that we have enclosed ourselves in four safe walls, but have forgotten to put a door in it. Our shelter has become a prison. We realize this when our way of dealing with life- our relationships, our stress, our anxieties- no longer works and we find that we are helpless, exhausted, and alone. When our way fails, this is God's way of revealing to us that we are imprisoned by our own will.

Our failures are allowed by God out of His mercy. When He reveals our imprisonment to us, and when we admit that we cannot manage our lives as well as we thought, we take the first step toward being set free. I think one of God's favorite prayers is when we say, "Lord, I can't do this anymore." He answers with, "Good, now that you have come to the end of your own strength, you can put yourself in my hands."

God uses this pain in our life to release our grip on the armor we have used for so long to protect ourselves. When we try to shut out pain, we shut Him out as well. But thanks to His grace, we can rejoice in our failures and thank Him because He is breaking our hold on the barrier that stands between us and His love. Because of His great love for us, He will not be shut out.

Over and over again in the book of Psalms, God shows that He is David's strong tower and refuge. For example, in Psalm 91:1,2 David declares, "He who dwells in the shelter of the Most High will rest in the shadow of the Almighty. I will say of the Lord, 'He is my refuge and my fortress, my God in whom I trust.'"

We do not have to build our own fortress, which ultimately becomes our prison, for God is our refuge, a very present help in time of trouble. He is the only one who can truly protect us and comfort us in life's pain and sorrow.

(Do a word study on refuge and fortress in Psalms. We don't have space here to list the rich promises you will find.)

The Unplowed Ground

The Bible speaks of hard, unfruitful ground to give us a picture of what our stubborn wills are like. In the book of Hosea, God tells us to "break up your unplowed ground; for it is time to seek the Lord." (Hosea 10:12). Our stubborn hearts separate us from Him.

Whether my will is a strong, independent, proud, unbending force, that grits its teeth and says, "I won't," or it is a whining, self-deprecating, self-pitying voice, whimpering, "I can't," my will is still in rebellion against God. It is resisting the Holy Spirit's will to make me more like Jesus Christ.

What are my greatest sins? Not my lusts, or passions, or addictions. Not my pride or emotions, or selfish ambition, or lying tongue. These are merely the foliage of the weed, but the root of the weed is my will. It pushes its way deep into my soul, where it holds tenaciously to its unseen home, and remains hidden and unchanged as it wields its power over me. It is unyielding in its grip, formidable in its strength, unequalled in its determination to survive. What does it matter to the root if some of the foliage is removed by my own attempts at self-improvement. My will, when it is not surrendered to God, is alive and well, and will continue to serve me from season to season.

Our High Priest

What was the last heart-rending prayer of our Lord before He went to the cross- His cries that reveal His humanity, that part of Him that enabled Him to identify with us, and now allows us to identify with Him? What was the last battle that had to be won, the ultimate example to us of obedience to God?

It was surrender to His Father's will.

He said, "Father, if you are willing, take this cup from me; yet not my will but yours be done." (Luke 22:42)

The battle in the garden of Gethsemane had to be won before the battle on the cross could be fought.

The will must be surrendered, before sin will die.

He did this so that He could become our High Priest, "who had to be made like His brothers in every way in order that He might become a merciful high priest in service to God. Because He Himself suffered when He was tempted, He is able to help those who are being tempted." (Hebrews 2:17, 18) We do not have a high priest who is unable to sympathize with our weaknesses, but we have one who has been tempted in every way, just as we are, yet was without sin" (Hebrews 4:15)

He drank the cup of death to the dregs. There was no other pain He could have learned, no added agony He could have experienced, no more excruciating suffering He could have endured that would have made Him more qualified to be the High Priest that we need.

Oh to know such a merciful Savior, who died for me. Why

do I not let Him have control of my will, that one part of me that separates me from Him-His love, His peace, His goodness.

Just as God tore the veil in the temple that separated us from His awesome, holy presence, may we pray that He will also tear the veil of our stubborn will that fights against His grace, rebels against His Lordship, and builds a fortress to shut out His conquering love.

He wants us to experience Him, not as an invading despot, but as our valiant hero, who breaks down every barrier, and defeats every foe that stands in the way of rescuing His maiden in distress.

Oh my sister in Christ, "let us then approach the throne of grace with confidence, so that we may receive mercy and find grace to help us in our time of need." (Hebrews 4:16)

PRAYER FOR THE WILLFUL "I"

There is a foe whose hidden power The Christian well may fear,
More subtle far than inbred sin And to the heart more dear.
It is the power of selfishness, it is the willful I,
And if ever my Lord can live in me My very self must die.
There is, like Anak's sons of old, A race of giant still,
Self-glorying, self-confidence Self-seeking and self-will.
Still must these haughty Anakim, by Caleb's sword be slain,
If ever Hebron's heights of heavenly love Our conquering feet can gain.
Oh, save me from self-will, dear Lord, Which claims Thy sacred Throne;
Oh, let my will be lost in Thine, and let Thy will be done.
Oh, keep me from self-confidence, and self-sufficiency;

Let me exchange my strength for Thine, and lean alone on Thee.
Oh, save me from self-seeking, Lord. Let me not be my own,
A living sacrifice I come--Lord, keep me Thine alone;
From proud vainglory save me, Lord. From pride of praise and fame;
To Christ be all the honor given, The glory to His name.
Oh Jesus, slay the Self in me, By thy consuming breath;
Show me thy heart, Thy wounds, Thy shame,
And love my soul to death.
When the Shekinah flame came down, E'en Moses could not say;
So let Thy glory fill me now, And self forever slay
Oh Jesus come and dwell in me, Walk in my steps each day,
Live in my life, love in my love, And speak in all I say;
Think in my thoughts, let all my acts, thy very actions be.
So shall it be no longer I, but Christ who lives in me.

A. B. Simpson

Take It To Heart:

"I have been crucified with Christ and I no longer live, but Christ lives in me. The life I live in the body, I live by faith in the Son of God, who loved me and gave Himself for me."

(Galatians 2:2:20)

CHAPTER 10

Tunnel Of Love

"I am my beloved's and my beloved is mine.
My beloved spoke and said to me,
'Arise my darling, my beautiful one,
Come with me'" Song of Solomon 6:3a; 2;10

The Wishing Well

Snow White made a wish at the wishing well, and as she did she sang these words, "I'm wishing for the one I love to find me, today. I'm hoping and I'm dreaming of the nice things he'll say."

As women we can all identify with Snow White's wish. It seems that wishing comes as natural to girls as breathing. We wish we were tall, or thin or beautiful, or rich, or smart. We wish our hair were long or short, blonde or brown, straight or curly. We wish we were more athletic, or talented or organized or successful. We wish our skin was younger and our kids were older. We wish our problems were smaller and our diamonds were bigger. I can remember that I was only in kindergarten when I realized my feet were ugly and my ankles were fat. I would wish mine were like the little girl's who walked in front of me on the way to recess. No one had to tell me to think this. It came naturally. Why? Because I was a girl!

As little girls, I'm sure that the lyrics of Snow White's song expressed our heart's desire. We looked forward to being loved by a dream-guy who would find us and say nice things to us, and love us unendingly.

As we grew up, our wishes became a little more sophisticated, but our tendency to wish remained. We wish for a happy marriage, a beautiful home, wonderful children, meaningful relationships, successful endeavors, and a fulfillment of all our dreams for the good life. Often those wishes come in the form of wishing we were like someone we see, or know, and the wishing becomes envy. We wish our husband was thoughtful and romantic, like someone else's, or our home was as pretty as another, or our children were as talented as our friends' children. Somehow we believe that if we could have our wishes, we would be happier than we are.

As I have gotten older, I have realized the foolishness of wishing. It is as foolish as throwing a penny down a well and believing that the wish will come true. It is time spent in thinking thoughts that will never accomplish anything. However, we continue to wish any way. We all want certain circumstances about our lives to be different. We have a yearning for perfect bliss, uninterrupted happiness, and an absolute absence of hardship, and heartache. Psychologists call it fantasizing. Why? Because what we wish for is a fantasy, a dream from our imagination, an escape from what we know undeniably to be reality. In our dreams, we always see things as being ideal for our sakes. As one wise saying states, "Illusions are dangerous things because they have no flaws."

I believe there is a reason why we have an insatiable desire for perfection, a yearning for a life of pure joy and peace, where we are loved eternally, and cared for completely. I believe that this desire is the last vestige of man's existence in the Garden of Eden. When God banished Adam and Eve from the garden, He did not erase their knowledge of God's plan, His beauty, and

His perfection. That knowledge is put there to drive us back to Him, to call out to Him in our distress, to recognize our need for Him. Why is it that we instinctively know that pain is not normal, heartache is not good, and cruelty is universally evil. If there were no such thing as perfect love, vibrant joy, and delicious peace, we would never be able to conceive of it. And we would never seek it, or try to make it happen in our lives. God uses those dreams of a perfect place to show us that the world is sinful and lost without Him. Without this unexplainable yearning for a better place, we would never hunger for heaven and for God. This world would be all that we would look to for our happiness.

Unfortunately, for most people, this world <u>is</u> all that they look to for happiness. Throughout history, since the Tower of Babel, the human race has believed that man can achieve a utopian existence through countless ways other than through God. Man is believed to be basically good by nature, and that, under the right conditions, man's achievements and intelligence are the answer to all social problems. They look to this world to satisfy their desires. But the Bible teaches that man is lost without the one true God, the Creator of all. Mankind is living in darkness, separated from God because of sin.

For those who have come to Christ in faith, believing that He is our salvation, we know that He is our only hope. We know that we live in a fallen world, that this earth is not our home, and that our home is in Heaven with God.

The writer of Psalm 84 knew this truth when wrote<u>, "How lovely is your dwelling place O Lord Almighty! My soul yearns, even faints, for the courts of the Lord; My heart and flesh cry out for the living God. (Psalm 84:1,2)</u>

Psalm 73:25 asks, "Whom have I in heaven, but you? And earth has nothing I desire besides you."

Solomon, the wisest man that ever lived, had all that he could wish for come true. He undertook great projects, built houses and gardens, owned flocks and herds, amassed silver and gold for himself, had a harem and all the delights of the heart of man.

He denied himself nothing his eyes desired; he refused his heart no pleasure. (Ecclesiastes 2) After having all his wishes come true, he ends with this conclusion, "When I surveyed all that my hands had done and what I had toiled to achieve, everything was meaningless, a chasing after the wind; nothing was gained under the sun." (Ecclesiastes 2:4-11)

And yet we keep on wishing.

As Christians, what does God want us to do? How does He want our thinking to change, if it is so foolish and pointless? The word of God teaches us that it is not our desire for that perfect bliss that is wrong. Rather, it is the belief that this world holds the answer apart from God. We look to the wrong things to satisfy our deepest desires. We have His image indelibly imprinted on our hearts, we have eternity embedded in our souls; we have His indwelling Holy Spirit, who is a "deposit guaranteeing our inheritance." (Ephesians 1:14) Therefore, God wants us to "set our hearts on things above, where Christ is seated at the right hand of God." We are to "set our minds on things above, not on earthly things. For you died (your old ways died when you received Christ as your savior), and your life is now hidden with Christ in God." (Colossians 3:1-3)

Our desires for that perfect place of love and joy and peace are not an impossible, unrealistic, foolish fantasy. They hold the promise of a dream that will become a reality, not in this life, but in the future in Heaven, when God resurrects us and makes all things new.

Yes, I am wishing for the One who loves me to find me. I am dreaming of that first moment I will behold His beautiful face, and gaze into the tender eyes of the One whom I have talked to, but only known dimly through a curtain. I know I will hear Him speaking to me- the "nice things He will say"-words of sacrificial, unconditional love, and incomparable joy at being together forever. I am anticipating that day when He will take me to that place He is preparing for me, where I will live with Him for eternity.

And that is not wishful thinking, or pointless dreaming. It is reality.

Where Do I Go From Here?

As little girls, we started making wishes, searching for love, and dreaming of happiness as soon as we were old enough to have a self-concept. Until God gets a hold of us, we are determined to find our dream and make it come true.

Then God shows us our need of Him, and slowly changes our independent will and our selfish ways.

God's love is the only thing that can break my will and conquer my stubborn heart. Paul referred to this when he "considered that our present sufferings are not worth comparing with the glory that will be revealed in us." (Romans 8:18) The peace and joy we can experience in this life, and the glory we will share in Heaven make us able to rejoice in the painful trials God allows in our lives. When we see that He works in us because He loves us, then we can surrender to Him.

Now when our soul competes with God for its own way, when we get frustrated at life, and discouraged in our circumstances, we know where to go-to the foot of the cross, where we can leave our sins, where forgiveness flows like the precious blood that was shed there. We can come boldly to the throne of grace, where we can find mercy and help in our time of need. We can drink from the well of Living Water, which, if we drink, we will never thirst again. We can come to Jesus Christ, who will give us rest and we will find peace for our souls.

Tunnel of Love

In the old days, an amusement park was a romantic place, where lovers would find romantic places to be alone and sneak a kiss, or whisper a sweet nothing in each other's ear. Sometimes they stood at the wishing well, and then ask each other what they wished, in hopes that the other's wish was for requited love. Sometimes, they engraved their initials, enclosed in a heart, on a giant oak tree. But the most romantic place to go was the tunnel of love. It was a place that was hidden, quiet, and intimate, away from the noises and stares of the crowd. Only those who were in love would want to go there together.

Jesus is our Lover, our Bridegroom, our Husband. We are His beloved, His bride. He is looking forward to that day when we will be with Him in His presence, and see Him face to face. We will behold His glory, and see with our own eyes, the One we have talked to and believed in and followed by faith, not by sight.

While we are on this earth, He is preparing us for Heaven. He is working in our hearts to love Him more and more. Paul prayed that we "being rooted and established in love, may have power, together with all the saints, to grasp how wide and long and high and deep is the love of Christ and to know this love that surpasses knowledge- that [we] may be filled to the measure of all the fullness of God." (Ephesians 3:18, 19)

When I can understand how He works in me, and the purpose of my trials, it gives me hope-hope that there is a purpose, hope that His purpose is for my good, hope that the trials are temporary (hallelujah!), and hope that I am being made new.

The Lord gave me a visual lesson of this principle.

At the time, I had six children-five boys ranging in ages from 15 years old to 3, and a baby daughter. At this stage of motherhood I was extremely tired! I used to wonder if there would ever be a day in my life again when I would know what it meant to not be tired! But I knew God's comfort and presence in my life, and had learned to trust that His plan for my life was good.

On this particular day, I was aware of how I was struggling to manage the bare essentials of my day. I was weary and discouraged and wanted a break. I slumped down in a chair and hung my head down in fatigue. Since my head was already bowed, I decided I might as well pray (but not because I was feeling very spiritual!). I decided to tell the Lord how I was feeling, so I sighed and sputtered, "Lord, I just feel like I need to see a light at the end of the tunnel."

As clear and real as my own thought was, a voice in my mind spoke to me, "I am the tunnel."

My heart stopped. My mind froze. My thoughts came to an abrupt halt.

The great I AM had spoken to me! The one who had spoken to Moses and said, "I AM WHO I AM."

The one who said, "I am the Bread of Life." (John 6:35)

The one who said, "I am the Way, the Truth, and the Life." (John 14:6)

The one who said, "I am the Resurrection and the Life." (John 11:25)

And what power His words had! What life! What comfort!

Suddenly, I realized that I was not trapped in a dark tunnel, but was hidden in the shadow of His wings. (Psalm 57:1b) In this place of isolation and difficulty, He was enclosing me in His presence, and sheltering me from the distractions and temporary solutions the world could offer. There He revealed His goodness and love to me in a way that I could never have known if I had not been in "the tunnel." He knew that I did not need to see a light at the end of the tunnel. I needed to see "Who" the tunnel was and why I was inside it.

I was in the Tunnel of Love, where it was quiet, secluded, and intimate; where I could hear the still, small voice of the One who loved me and was drawing me closer to His heart.

As He and I have come out of the tunnel and into the brilliant sunshine of hope and joy, I have found that He continues to set me free from my old ways that prevent me from knowing His Love.

"If the Son sets you free, you will be free indeed!"(John 8:36)

I want to tell you, dear sister in Christ, that I have learned that God's purpose in changing us so deeply and completely, although painfully, is so that we can experience His amazing love and peace. It is in the tunnel, the dark places of our lives, that we sense His quiet but strong and powerful presence, alone with us in that place. His arms gently enfold us in His embrace, where we can lay our head against His heart and know that at last we have found the love and peace we have been searching for all of our lives.

Take It To Heart:

"Come to me, all you who are weary and burdened, and I will give you rest. Take my yoke upon you and learn from me, for I am gentle and humble in heart, and you will find rest for your souls. For my yoke is easy and my burden is light." (Matthew 11:28-30)

CONCLUSION

This book began with the idea that we are each a heroine in God's story about Himself. God is a lover of stories. The most sublime story ever told is the story of the God who became a man and dwelt among us so that we could be brought back to God. God has wired us to be moved by stories. That is how He communicates with His creatures.

In Psalm 139, David talks to God of this amazing life he lives with his God. "O Lord, you have searched me and you know me. You know when I sit and when I rise. You perceive my thoughts from afar. You discern my going out and my lying down; You are familiar with all my ways. Before a word is on my tongue you know it completely, O Lord. You hem me in-behind and before; you have laid your hand upon me. Such knowledge is too wonderful for me, too lofty for me to attain. All the days ordained for me were written in your book before one of them came to be." (Psalm 139:1-6, 16)

David knew that God was writing a story of his life to show us what God is like. And he recorded it so that we could know that our life is a story also. Another man in the Bible, who loved the power of the story, was the Apostle John. His gospel is considered to be one of the most beautiful pieces of literature in human history. The last sentence of his gospel speaks to us again about the power of stories. "Jesus also did many other things. If they were all written down, I suppose the whole world could not contain the books that would be written." (John 21:25)

Yes God will keep writing stories about His love, and His beloved Son and His people as long as there are people on this earth. God wants you to know that you were created to be an essential part of His story. You are not an isolated individual, just trying to figure out how to live, what to do, and where to go in order to find fulfillment in some vague purpose. No, you were created for an eternal purpose that is bigger than yourself. You, with your heart, your personality, your gifts, your dreams, and your values, are

~ a hand-carved piece of a Divine Puzzle, or
~ an exquisite thread in the Grand Tapestry, or
~ a lustrous color on the Master's Canvas, or
~ a sweet musical note in the Symphony of Heaven.

And no one can take your place.

Will you let Him rule your heart, and believe that He has given you the heart of a heroine?

Imagine what your story will be.